David Hartnell ha[...] long as he can re[...] his regular radio [...] newspaper colum[...] Zealand have continued in the tradition of the great Hollywood gossip writers, bringing informative gossip and scandal of extravagant lifestyles to his ever-ready readers and listeners.

Brian Williams was born in England and first saw Hollywood in the 1980s. He was immediately hooked, and loves to expose the Hollywood star system with his sense of humour, acute observation and first-class memory.

I'M NOT ONE TO GOSSIP, BUT ...

Tinseltown Trivia from Hollywood's Premier
Celebrity Spotter

David Hartnell and Brian Williams

Futura

A Futura Book

First published in Great Britain by Futura Publications, a Division of Macdonald & Co (Publishers) Ltd, London & Sydney

Copyright © David Hartnell, 1990

ALL RIGHTS RESERVED

No part of this publication may be reproduced, stored in a retrieval system, or transmitted, in any form or by any means without the prior permission in writing of the publisher, nor be otherwise circulated in any form of binding or cover other than that in which it is published and without a similar condition including this condition being imposed on the subsequent purchaser.

Printed and bound in Great Britain by
BPCC Hazell Books
Aylesbury, Bucks, England
Member of BPCC Ltd.

ISBN 0 7088 4843 5

Futura Publications
A Division of
Macdonald & Co (Publishers) Ltd
Orbit House
1 New Fetter Lane
London EC4A 1AR
A member of Maxwell Macmillan Pergamon Publishing Corporation

Acknowledgements

Firstly, we would like to thank Steve Wright, Managing Director of Macdonald Publishers (NZ) for accepting this book on our very first meeting, and also to Michael Hooper for introducing us.

Our gratitude to every star who appears within these pages, for without their flamboyant and bizarre lifestyles we would have no material at all! Many thanks to Alice Worsley, Max Cryer, John Parker, Fran Zell, Robin Harrison, Kathleen Smitheram, George Balani, Grahame Cox, Georginna Francisco, Susan Sweeny, Bob Leahy, Darlene Russell and Kevan Moore; for their encouragement and ideas when putting this book together.

To Phyllis Diller for writing the foreword, and for her extra special friendship over the past thirty years.

And finally, a very special thanks to Matthew West for all the gossiping and good times we have spent together in Hollywood over the years.

This book is lovingly dedicated to Alice May Williams of Brentwood, California.
Without her friendship, love and encouragement over the years, this book could never have been written.

Thanks ... You're one in a million!

Contents

Foreword	x
Introduction	1
1 The Stars Are Born – When and Where	3
2 What's in a Name?	9
3 Love, Marriage and Divorce, Hollywood Style	25
4 Brief Biographies	35
5 Sports, Games and Hobbies of the Stars	53
6 In Which They Served: Military and other connections	59
7 Family Ties	63
8 Home Sweet Home	75
9 Debuts	79
10 Music, Music, Music – and Musicians	88
11 The Small Screen	101
12 The Ones that Got Away: Roles they turned down	115
13 Unexpected Appearances	127
14 Good Luck Charms	132
15 Tinseltown	135
16 Making Their Mark: The Walk of Fame, etc.	144
17 Money, Money, Money – or lack of it	148
18 Stars in Print	163
19 What They Did Before, and After	172
20 Intimate Details	184
21 Hollywood Wit	194
22 Firsts	207
23 Westerns	210

24 Cartoons	213
25 Four-Legged Friends	217
26 Oscars, and Other Awards	221
27 Getting Technical	236
28 Whoops!	241
29 Exits	246
30 Everything You Ever Wanted to Know ...	258

Foreword

It is fitting and proper that a dyed-in-the-wool Hollywoodite should write the foreword to David and Brian's book. I have known David since the Cave Age, and have approved of Brian ever since I met him at a sheep-shearing event in New Zealand.

This book will scatter wit and semi-wisdom in all my favourite English-speaking countries of the world.

This perfectly funny and lovely tome which David and Brian put together will give you titters, giggles and some really bizarre information. And it's *all* true!

Phyllis Diller

9 December 1989

Beverly Wilshire Hotel

I'm not one to gossip but ... HOLLYWOOD is a city where the lights never go out, and the volume knob is always turned up full. Everybody comes to Hollywood hoping to win that pot of solid gold, willing to risk everything to realise their dream. A few succeed where thousands fail.

Often the pressures at the top of the Hollywood ladder can be the same as the pain felt at the bottom. Cybill Shepherd once told me, 'Hollywood is the only city in the world where you can climb to the top of the success ladder, and still get stabbed in the back!'

Hollywood is a city where it all comes down to one eight letter word: *survival*! From the very first day Hollywood came about, there have always been dramas – booze, drugs, tragedies, scandals, gossip, and movie star legends. Hollywood stars have made us sing, laugh and cry, we've named our children after them, dressed like them and even their problems have become our concerns.

To be called a 'star' here in Hollywood means you've really made it! Let's face it, we wouldn't have HOLLYWOOD any other way. So it's still hooray for Hollywood!

David H.W. Hartnell

Wilshire Boulevard at Rodeo Drive, Beverly Hills, California 90212

The Stars Are Born
- When and Where

When Clark Gable was born on 1st February 1901 in Ohio, he was mistakenly listed as a female on his birth certificate. He originally spelt his name Clarke Gabel.

☆

Ballet dancer Rudolf Nureyev was born on a train.

☆

When Humphrey Bogart joined the Warner Bros. Studio, they changed his birth date to Christmas Day 1899, thinking this would add glamour. In fact he was born on 23rd January 1899.

☆

Barbara Bel Geddes, who plays Miss Ellie in 'Dallas', was born on 21st October 1922; Larry Hagman, who plays JR, was born on 21st September 1931. This means that Miss Ellie would have been only nine years old when JR was born.

☆

The true dates of birth of the Gabor sisters are thought to be: Magda, 10th July 1917; Zsa Zsa, 6th February 1919; Eva, 11th February 1921; and their mother, Jolie Gabor, 29th September 1896. Zsa Zsa once gave a Hollywood press conference to settle the question of her age for good. She produced a birth certificate which stated she was fifty-four years old. But one columnist worked out that she would have been only thirteen when she married her first husband, Burhan Belge, a powerful super-rich Turkish foreign affairs minister. In fact Zsa Zsa was well out of her teens on her first wedding day.

☆

Elizabeth Taylor's parents were American, but she was born in London on 27th February 1932.

☆

Bianca Jagger, ex-wife of Rolling Stone Mick, was born in Nicaragua.

☆

Rod Steiger is a year younger than Marlon Brando, yet he played Marlon's elder brother in *On the Waterfront* (1954).

☆

James Cagney was born in 1899, but Warner Bros. Studio moved his birth date forward five years to 1904, to cash in on his baby-faced appearance.

☆

Donald Duck was born in 1934.

☆

Kings of the horror movies Christopher Lee, Peter Cushing and Vincent Price all share the same birthday, 27th May.

☆

Johnny Cash, Cher, James Garner and Burt Reynolds are all part Cherokee.

☆

Audrey Hepburn was born in Belgium.

☆

Cole Porter and Harpo Marx were good friends; they were both born in 1893 and died in the same year, 1964.

☆

Julie Christie was born in India.

☆

Here is a list of stars who were born in Canada, not the US, as is generally supposed: Yvonne de Carlo, Marie Dressler, Deanna Durbin, Michael J. Fox, John Ireland, Ruby Keeler, Gene Lockhart, Raymond Massey, Barbara Parkins, Mary Pickford, Walter Pidgeon, Christopher Plummer, William Shatner, Norma Shearer, Alexis Smith, Donald Sutherland, Fay Wray.

☆

Rock Hudson was born in 1925, but his agent added two years to his age so he would get more mature roles.

☆

In *Indiana Jones and the Last Crusade* Sean Connery played Harrison Ford's father. Since Sean was born in 1930 and Harrison in 1942, Sean was only twelve years old when Harrison was born.

☆

British actor Peter Ustinov is of Russian and Ethiopian descent.

☆

It's often stated that actor Sam Neill was born in New Zealand. In fact he was born in Ireland and emigrated to New Zealand with his parents at the age of seven. His real name is Nigel Neil, but his parents nicknamed him Sam as a baby and the name stuck.

☆

In *Yankee Doodle Dandy* (1942) Rosemary de Camp played James Cagney's mother, yet in real life she was fourteen years his junior.

☆

Al Jolson, Irving Berlin and George Sanders were all born in Russia. They met when their show business careers crossed in America.

☆

Jack Lemmon was born in a hospital lift.

☆

Sarah Miles, the actress, and singer John Denver were both born on New Year's Eve in 1943.

☆

Dorothy Faye Dunaway was born on a peanut farm in Bascom, Florida, on 14th January 1941. Her father John was a US Army sergeant and her mother Grace a devout Methodist.

☆

Although America claims him as her very own, Bob Hope was born in England.

☆

Sidney Poitier was a premature baby and weighed just three pounds at birth.

☆

Actress/singer Olivia Newton-John was born in England, not in Australia as is often thought.

☆

American actress Victoria Principal was born in Japan.

☆

Debbie Reynolds was born on April Fool's Day 1932, in El Paso, Texas.

☆

In 1942 Greer Garson played the title role in *Mrs Miniver*. A couple of years later Greer married Richard Ney, who played her son in the movie.

☆

Basil Rathbone was born in South Africa.

☆

Horror king Bela Lugosi, who frequently played the Count from Transylvania, was actually born in Transylvania.

☆

Joan Blondell lived in Australia until she was eighteen, then headed for Hollywood and an acting career.

☆

Stan Laurel was born on 16th June 1890 in Ulverston, which now boasts the only museum totally dedicated to Laurel and Hardy memorabilia.

☆

Actress Olivia Hussey was born in Argentina.

☆

Patrick McGowan, star of the 1960s cult TV series 'The Prisoner', was not English; he was born in New York.

☆

For years Merle Oberon insisted she was born in Tasmania, but this was not true. She was born in Bombay of a Sinhalese mother and brought up in India. This fact was guarded until just after her death; had it got out in the early days of her career, it would have been over before it started, as interracial romance was a taboo matter.

What's in a Name?

A Hollywood star must have the right kind of name – one the public will remember, that looks good in lights, a name that's not too long, or difficult to pronounce, or simply unglamorous. Here's how some stars got their names.

☆

Richard Burton, born Richard Jenkins, was the last of thirteen children born to a Welsh coal miner in the unpronounceable hamlet of Pontrhydfen. At school his drama coach, Phillip Burton, took young Jenkins under his wing, and later in life Richard assumed his mentor's name.

☆

Shirley MacLaine says her mother was such a fan of Shirley Temple that she was named after her.

☆

Joseph Keaton got the nickname 'Buster' when he was six years old. He fell downstairs, and Harry Houdini, a family friend, said to his father, 'That was some buster he took falling down the stairs.' Little did Harry know he had just named one of the greatest comic stars ever.

☆

Some stars have added an extra letter or two to their birth names.
Dionne Warwicke added an 'e' to her last name;
Lauren Bacall added an 'l' to her last name;
Rita Hayworth added the 'y';
Vivien Leigh's first name was originally spelt with an 'a'.
Stage manager Sydney Carroll thought changing it to an 'e' would make her appear more feminine to her fans;
Barbra Streisand dropped an 'a' from Barbara;
Carole Lombard added the 'e';
Audry Hepburn-Ruston added an 'e' to her first name and dropped Ruston;
Irene Dunne added an 'e' to her last name;
Warren Beatty added a 't'.

☆

It was a man called Gordon Mills who turned Raymond O'Sullivan into Gilbert O'Sullivan, Thomas Jones Woodward into Tom Jones and Arnold Dorsey into Engelbert Humperdinck. Arnold was the ninth of ten children born to a British Army officer who was stationed in Madras, India, when Arnold was born.

☆

Some cartoon characters have also started life with a different name. Mickey Mouse was born Mortimer Mouse; Goofy was first known as Dippy Dawg; Happy Rabbit changed his name to Bugs Bunny and Tom, of *Tom and Jerry* fame, was first named Jasper.

☆

Actress Mariel Hemingway was named after a bay in Cuba.

☆

Paul was the real name of the original Lassie, and every Lassie since has been given the nickname Paul.

☆

Elton John, born Reg Dwight, took his stage name from two of his friends, Elton Dean and Long John Baldry, whom he played with in a band in grammar school. He was the very first superstar to admit to being bisexual.

☆

Conway Twitty created his stage name by combining the names of towns in Arkansas and Texas.

☆

Bette Davis was nearly given the name Betting Dawes by a Hollywood agent.

☆

Top Italian model Sofia Scicolone was later to become actress Sophia Loren.

☆

It took Carol Jane Peters quite a while to come up with a star quality name. She was sitting in a coffee shop when she looked across the road and spotted a pharmacy called Lombardi Pharmacy on Lexington Avenue and 65th Street in New York. And so the actress Carole Lombard was born.

☆

In his early vaudeville days George Burns worked under the names of Willie Delight, Captain Belts and Buddy Links.

☆

In the 1930s and 40s it was very fashionable to have a middle initial, a trend followed by quite a few movie directors of the day. Here's what their middle initials stood for: Cecil Blount DeMille; David Oliver Selznick; Louis Burt Mayer; Darryl Francis Zanuck; Irving Grant Thalberg.

☆

Wladziu Valentino Liberace used the name Walter Buster Keys at the start of his piano-playing career; but later changed it to Liberace.

☆

American radio announcer Bob Smith thought his name was far too boring, so in the 1960s he changed it to Wolfman Jack, and he's never looked back.

☆

Some hopeful stars changed their Christian names into surnames; for example, Allen Stewart Konigsberg became Woody Allen and Malden Sekulovich became Karl Malden. Some dropped their first names:

(Clarence)	Robert Cummings
(Ruth)	Bette Davis
(Sari)	Zsa Zsa Gabor
(Norvell)	Oliver Hardy
(Leslie)	Bob Hope
(Julius)	Groucho Marx
(James)	David Niven

(Marilyn)	Kim Novak
(Julia)	Lana Turner
(William)	Clark Gable
(Edward)	Montgomery Clift
(Terence)	Steve McQueen
(Patrick)	Ryan O'Neal
(Eldred)	Gregory Peck
(Edith)	Norma Shearer
(Ernestine)	Jane Russell

☆

In 1925 the MGM studios held a nationwide contest to rename their latest starlet find, Lucille Le Sueur. Well over 20,000 names were sent in, and the winner chose the name Joan Arden. The studio liked the name, but later found out they already had an actress signed up whose real name was Joan Arden, and so Lucille's name was changed to Joan Crawford.

☆

Dustin Hoffman's mother was a great fan of the silent cowboy movie star Dustin Farnum, who starred in the first full-length movie ever made in Hollywood. That's where Dustin gets his name from.

☆

Walter Matuschanskayasky renamed himself Walter Matthau, but in 'Earthquake' (1974), where he played a cameo role as a drunk, he was billed as Walter Matuschanskayasky for a laugh.

☆

Actress Swoosie Kurtz was named after a B-17 World War II plane which her father flew.

Francis Rose Shore took her stage name, 'Dinah', from the song of the same name which was suggested to her by Eddie Cantor while she was working on his radio show.

☆

Lauren Bacall's mother, Natalie Weinstein, changed her name to Bacal because it means wineglass in Romanian. Later Lauren added the extra 'l'.

☆

Have you ever wondered how River Pheonix, the young Hollywood actor, got his name? His parents were hippies in the 1960s and named him after the River of Life in Hermann Hesse's book *Siddhartha*. They took their surname, Phoenix, from the mythical bird which burnt itself but rose from the ashes to live again. Incidentally River's brothers and sisters also have names reminiscent of flower-power days; Leaf, Rainbow, Summer and Liberty.

☆

When they were making the first *Jaws* movie, the cast and crew nicknamed the shark Bruce, a name which stuck through all the sequels.

☆

Tadeus Wladyslaw Konopka changed his name to Ted Knight in 1947 by picking a name out of the LA phone directory. He was careful to select a name with the same initials as his own, so that he didn't have to change his luggage.

☆

It was just as well that British James Stewart decided to change his name to Stewart Granger before American James Stewart got into movies.

☆

Maurice Joseph Micklewhite got his stage name from the movie *The Caine Mutiny*. We know him as Michael Caine.

☆

Some early Hollywood stars became so famous that they were known by their nicknames:

Bing Crosby:	the Groaner
Clara Bow:	the 'It' Girl
Frank Sinatra:	Ol' Blue Eyes
Betty Grable:	the Pin-Up Girl
Jimmy Durante:	the Shnozz
Rita Hayworth:	the Love Goddess
Jeanette MacDonald:	the Iron Butterfly
Bob Hope:	Ski-Nose
John Wayne:	Duke
Clark Gable:	the King of Hollywood
Veronica Lake:	the Peek-a-boo Girl
Charlie Chaplin:	the Little Tramp
Lana Turner:	the Sweater Girl
Dorothy Lamour:	the Sarong Girl
Carmen Miranda:	the Brazilian Bombshell
Jean Harlow:	the Platinum Blonde
Greta Garbo:	the Sphinx
Rudolph Valentino:	the Sheik
Doris Day:	the Professional Virgin

☆

Glen Ford, born Gwyllen Ford, named himself after his father's birthplace in Canada – a little Quebec town called Glenford.

☆

Doris von Kappellhof was named Doris Day by bandleader Barney Rapp, whose favourite song was 'Day After Day', which Doris had sung many times with the band.

☆

Roy Scherer had his name changed to Rock Hudson by his agent Henry Wilson: Rock after the Rock of Gibraltar, and Hudson after the mighty river in New York.

☆

Harry Crosby came up with his movie name 'Bing', remembering the comic strip he always read as a child, *The Bingville Bugle*.

☆

Actress Judy Holliday was born Judith Tuvim. The word *tuvim* in Hebrew means holiday.

☆

One German comedian changed his name to Charlie Kaplin, and became a much loved comic in Germany. Charlie Chaplin tried to sue him, but failed. A movie actor in Hong Kong changed his name to Bruce Li, and is now finding fame and a lot of fortune following in the footsteps of the late Bruce Lee.

☆

Most people know that John Wayne's real name was Marion Michael Morrison, but the name on his birth certificate is Marion Robert Morrison.

☆

Movie mogul Sam Goldwyn was born Samuel Goldfish.

☆

The Marx brothers all took their first names from a comic strip called *Mager's Monks*.

☆

American actor Bud Flanagan thought his name was terrible and lacked star quality, so he changed it to Dennis O'Keefe. Miles away in London, British actor Robert Winthrop changed his name to Bud Flanagan. They did not know each other.

☆

Is it any wonder that Rudolpho Alfonzo Raffaelo Pierre Filibert Guglielmi di Valentino d'Antonguolla changed his name to Rudolph Valentino?

☆

Marilyn Monroe got her Christian name from her 20th Century-Fox agent Ben Lyon, because of his admiration for the actress Marilyn Miller. Monroe was her mother's maiden name.

☆

Little Frances Gumm selected her stage surname from the pages of a Chicago newspaper, where she read reviews by Robert Garland. She took her first name from the Hoagy Carmichael song 'Judy', which was one of her favourites.

☆

Here is a list of other actors who worked under stage names, and their original names:

Eddie Albert:	Edward Albert Heimberger
Robert Alda:	Alphonso Giovanni Guiseppe Roberto
Jane Alexander:	Jane Quigley
Fred Allen:	John Florence Sullivan
Julie Andrews:	Julia Elizabeth Wells
Eve Arden:	Eunice Quedens
Beatrice Arthur	Bernice Frankel
Jean Arthur:	Gladys Georgianna Greene
Fred Astaire:	Frederick Austerlitz
Anne Bancroft:	Anna Maria Italiano
Brigitte Bardot:	Camille Javal
Gene Barry:	Eugene Klass
Pat Benatar:	Patricia Andrejewski
Robbie Benson:	Robert Segal
Tony Bennett:	Anthony Benedetto
Busby Berkeley:	William Berkeley Enos
Jack Benny:	Benjamin Kubelsky
Joey Bishop:	Joseph Gottlieb
Robert Blake:	Michael Gubitosi
Victor Borge:	Borge Rosenbaum
David Bowie:	David Robert Jones
Boy George:	George Alan O'Dowd
Fanny Brice:	Fanny Borach
Morgan Brittany:	Suzanne Cupito

Charles Bronson:	Charles Buchinski
Albert Brooks:	Albert Einstein
Mel Brooks:	Melvin Kaminsky
George Burns:	Nathan Birnbaum
Ellen Burstyn:	Edna Gilhooley
Red Buttons:	Aaron Chwatt
Nicolas Cage:	Nicholas Coppola
Maria Callas:	Maria Kalogeropoulos
Diahann Carroll:	Carol Diahann Johnson
Cyd Charisse:	Tula Finklea
Ray Charles:	Ray Charles Robinson
Cher:	Cherilyn Sarkisian
Patsy Cline:	Virginia Patterson Hensley
Lee J. Cobb:	Leo Jacoby
Claudette Colbert:	Lily Chauchoin
Michael Connors:	Kreker Ohanian
Robert Conrad:	Conrad Robert Falk
Alice Cooper:	Vincent Furnier
Elvis Costello:	Declan Patrick McManus
Lou Costello:	Louis Cristillo
Tony Curtis:	Bernard Schwartz
Vic Damone:	Vito Farinola
Rodney Dangerfield:	Jacob Cohen
Bobby Darin:	Walden Waldo Cassotto
Yvonne De Carlo:	Peggy Middleton
Sandra Dee:	Alexandra Zuck
John Denver:	Henry John Deutschendorf Jr.
Bo Derek:	Cathleen Collins
John Derek:	Derek Harris
Angie Dickinson:	Angeline Brown
Phyllis Diller:	Phyllis Driver
Diana Dors:	Diana Fluck

Melvyn Douglas:	Melvyn Hesselberg
Bob Dylan:	Robert Zimmerman
Sheena Easton:	Sheena Shirley Orr
Barbara Eden:	Barbara Huffman
Ron Ely:	Ronald Pierce
Chad Everett:	Raymond Cramton
Douglas Fairbanks:	Douglas Ullman
Morgan Fairchild:	Patsy McClenny
Alice Faye:	Ann Leppert
W.C. Fields:	William Claude Dukenfield
Peter Finch:	William Mitchell
Barry Fitzgerald:	William Joseph Shields
Joan Fontaine:	Joan de Havilland
John Ford:	Sean O'Feama
John Forsythe:	John Freund
Redd Foxx:	John Sanford
Anthony Franciosa:	Anthony Papaleo
Arlene Francis:	Arlene Kazanjian
Connie Francis:	Concetta Franconero
Greta Garbo:	Greta Gustafsson
Vincent Gardenia:	Vincent Scognamiglio
John Garfield:	Julius Garfinkle
James Garner:	James Baumgardner
Crystal Gayle:	Brenda Gayle Webb
Eydie Gorme:	Edith Gormezano
Stewart Granger:	James Stewart
Cary Grant:	Archibald Leach
Lee Grant:	Lyova Rosenthal
Joel Grey:	Joe Katz
Buddy Hackett:	Leonard Hacker
Jean Harlow:	Harlean Carpentier
Rex Harrison:	Reginald Carey

Laurence Harvey:	Larushka Skikne
Helen Hayes:	Helen Brown
Susan Hayward:	Edythe Marriner
Rita Hayworth:	Margarita Cansino
Pee-Wee Herman:	Paul Rubenfeld
Barbara Hershey:	Barbara Herzstine
William Holden:	William Beedle
Harry Houdini:	Ehrich Weiss
Leslie Howard:	Leslie Stainer
Rock Hudson:	Roy Scherer Jr. (later Fitzgerald)
Kim Hunter:	Janet Cole
Mary Beth Hurt:	Mary Supinger
Betty Hutton:	Betty Thornberg
David Janssen:	David Meyer
Don Johnson:	Donald Wayne
Jennifer Jones:	Phyllis Isley
Louis Jourdan:	Louis Gendre
Boris Karloff:	William Henry Pratt
Danny Kaye:	David Kaminsky
Diane Keaton:	Diane Hall
Michael Keaton:	Michael Douglas
Howard Keel:	Harold Leek
Chaka Khan:	Yvette Stevens
Carole King:	Carole Klein
Ben Kingsley:	Krishna Banji
Nastassja Kinski:	Nastassja Naksyznyski
Cheryl Ladd:	Cheryl Stoppelmoor
Veronica Lake:	Constance Ockleman
Dorothy Lamour:	Mary Kaumeyer
Michael Landon:	Eugene Orowitz
Mario Lanza:	Alfredo Cocozza
Stan Laurel:	Arthur Jefferson

Steve Lawrence:	Sidney Leibowitz
Brenda Lee:	Brenda Mae Tarpley
Bruce Lee:	Lee Yuen Kam
Gypsy Rose Lee:	Rose Louise Hovick
Michelle Lee:	Michelle Dusiak
Peggy Lee:	Norma Egstrom
Janet Leigh:	Jeanette Morrison
Vivien Leigh:	Vivian Hartley
Huey Lewis:	Hugh Cregg
Jerry Lewis:	Joseph Levitch
Hal Linden:	Harold Lipshitz
Jack Lord:	John Joseph Ryan
Peter Lorre:	Laszio Lowenstein
Myrna Loy:	Myrna Williams
Bela Lugosi:	Bela Ferenc Blasko
Shirley MacLaine:	Shirley Beaty
Madonna:	Madonna Louise Ciccone
Lee Majors:	Harvey Lee Yeary 2d
Jayne Mansfield:	Vera Jane Palmer
Fredric March:	Frederick Bickel
Peter Marshall:	Pierre LaCock
Dean Martin:	Dino Crocetti
Ethel Merman:	Ethel Zimmerman
Ray Milland:	Reginald Truscott-Jones
Ann Miller:	Lucille Collier
Joni Mitchell:	Roberta Joan Anderson
Marilyn Monroe:	Norma Jeane Mortenson
Yves Montand:	Ivo Levi
Demi Moore:	Demi Guynes
Rita Moreno:	Rosita Alverio
Harry Morgan:	Harry Bratsburg
Mike Nichols:	Michael Igor Peschowsky
Hugh O'Brian:	Hugh Krampke

Maureen O'Hara:	Maureen Fitzsimmons
Patti Page:	Clara Ann Fowler
Jack Palance:	Walter Palanuik
Lilli Palmer:	Lilli Peiser
Bert Parks:	Bert Jacobson
Minnie Pearl:	Sarah Ophelia Cannon
Bernadette Peters:	Bernadette Lazzaro
Edith Piaf:	Edith Gassion
Slim Pickens:	Louis Lindley
Mary Pickford:	Gladys Smith
Stephanie Powers:	Stefania Federkiewcz
Paula Prentiss:	Paula Ragusa
Robert Preston:	Robert Preston Merservey
Prince:	Prince Rogers Nelson
Tony Randall:	Leonard Rosenberg
Martha Raye:	Margaret O'Reed
Donna Reed:	Donna Belle Mullenger
Della Reese:	Delloreese Patricia Early
Joan Rivers:	Joan Sandra Molinsky
Edward G. Robinson:	Emanuel Goldenberg
Ginger Rogers:	Virginia McMath
Roy Rogers:	Leonard Slye
Mickey Rooney:	Joe Yule Jr.
Lillian Russell:	Helen Leonard
Susan St. James:	Susan Miller
Susan Sarandon:	Susan Tomaling
Randolph Scott:	George Randolph Crane
Jane Seymour:	Joyce Frankenberg
Omar Sharif:	Michael Shalhoub
Martin Sheen:	Ramon Estevez
Beverly Sills:	Belle Silverman
Phil Silvers:	Philip Silversmith
Suzanne Somers:	Suzanne Mahoney

Ann Sothern:	Harriette Lake
Barbara Stanwyck:	Ruby Stevens
Jean Stapleton:	Jeanne Murray
Ringo Starr:	Richard Starkey
Connie Stevens:	Concetta Ingolia
Donna Summers:	LaDonna Gaines
Robert Taylor:	Spangler Arlington Brugh
Sophie Tucker:	Sophia Kalish
Tina Turner:	Annie Mae Bullock
Conway Twitty:	Harold Lloyd Jenkins
Frankie Valli:	Frank Castelluccio
Clifton Webb:	Webb Parmalee Hollenbeck
Raquel Welch:	Raquel Tejada
Gene Wilder:	Jerome Silberman
Shelley Winters:	Shirley Schrift
Stevie Wonder:	Stevland Morris
Natalie Wood:	Natasha Gurdin
Jane Wyman:	Sarah Jane Fulks
Gig Young:	Byron Barr

Love, Marriage and Divorce, Hollywood Style

Warren Beatty has held the title of Hollywood Sex Symbol for more than twenty-five years. His romantic involvements had been well publicized in every gossip column, with just about every eligible woman in Tinseltown. Here are some of his better known celebrity dates over the years: Mary Tyler Moore, Jackie Onassis, Jane Fonda, Goldie Hawn, Faye Dunaway, Joan Collins, Catherine Deneuve, Britt Ekland, Diane Keaton, Kate Jackson, Joni Mitchell, Vivien Leigh, Vanessa Redgrave, Diana Ross, Jean Seberg, Madonna, Barbra Streisand, Elizabeth Taylor, Natalie Wood, Cher, Candice Bergen, Julie Christie, Brigitte Bardot. When Warren dumped singer/songwriter Carly Simon, she wrote the smash hit song 'You're So Vain' and dedicated it to him.

☆

John Travolta and Diana Hyland (who was eighteen years his senior) were a hot item around Hollywood; they had one of the most publicized affairs ever. It all ended tragically when she died in John's arms while he was filming *Saturday Night Fever* in 1976. He was only twenty-two at the time.

☆

Howard Hughes and Elizabeth Taylor became a dating twosome in Hollywood when she was only seventeen.

☆

Ethel Barrymore turned down Winston Churchill's proposal of marriage.

☆

Rita Hayworth was already pregnant with her daughter Princess Yasmin when she married Prince Aly Khan in 1949.

☆

George Sanders married Zsa Zsa Gabor in 1949 and divorced her in 1954. He again found love in the Gabor family and married her sister Magda in 1970. The marriage to Zsa Zsa, her third, lasted only six weeks. To this day Zsa Zsa says he was the love of her life. George once said of the marriage: 'Life with Zsa Zsa is like living on the slopes of a volcano. Very pleasant between eruptions.'

☆

In October 1977 actor John Ritter married actress Nancy Morgan. The morning after their wedding night John had an early start on his TV sitcom 'Three's Company', and as a protest at having to work while on honeymoon he turned up on the set in his pyjamas.

☆

When Diahann Carroll married her white talent manager, Monty Kay, her family were so shocked that her father would not attend the wedding, even though it was held at her family's church in Harlem.

☆

Jane Wyman may have missed out on being the White House's First Lady, but she is certainly 'Falcon Crest's First Lady, and very much the star of the show. She divorced her first husband, Myron Futterman, in 1937. While working on *Brother Rat* she met a handsome young actor called Ronald Reagan, and two years later, in 1940, they had a Hollywood wedding, at Forest Lawn Cemetery, in their Wee Kirk of the Heather church. They were divorced in 1949. In 1952 she married orchestra leader Freddie Karger. They were divorced in 1954, remarried in 1961 and redivorced in 1965. Over the years Jane has been philosophical about what might have been: 'I've no regrets about missing out on the White House. It's definitely not my scene. But I was delighted when Ronnie was elected. We have always remained friends, and I have so many wonderful memories of our life together.'

☆

Farrah Fawcett was known to American TV viewers long before 'Charlie's Angels' came along; they saw her selling more than 100 products, from Wella Balsam to Ulta Brite. During this time she met a handsome young pro football star turned actor, Lee Majors. They were married in 1973 but separated in 1979.

☆

Angie Dickinson, who starred in TV's 'Police Woman' was born Angeline Brown in Kulm, North Dakota. 'Dickinson' came from her marriage to American football star Gene Dickinson; they were married while still at college. Angie kept her married name and used it professionally, even while married to her second husband Burt Bacharach. She was once asked by a leading fashion magazine if she dressed for success. She replied, 'I dress for women – and I undress for men.'

☆

Katharine Hepburn was married in 1928 to Ludlow Ogden Smith, a wealthy French-educated Philadelphia socialite. Before she would marry him, she made him change his name to Ogden Ludlow so that she would not have to be known as Mrs Smith. Their marriage was short lived; they parted company soon after the honeymoon, but did not divorce until May 1934. When asked about her marriage by a reporter, Katharine said, 'Was I ever married? I really can't remember. It certainly wasn't for very long.' To this day she will not speak of her marriage.

☆

Robert Foxworth, who plays Chase Gioberti in 'Falcon Crest', is married to TV's 'Bewitched' star Elizabeth Montgomery.

☆

When Sophia Loren was co-starring with Cary Grant in *Houseboat* she flatly turned down a marriage proposal from him. Three years later to the very day she married Carlo Ponti who was twenty-one years her senior, not to mention four inches shorter. They were married in Mexico but the Italian government and the Vatican refused to recognize Carlo's Mexican divorce from his wife. During the following nine years he spent some $2 million in legal fees so that they could become French citizens and remarry under French law.

☆

Mel Gibson is very much a married man; he and his wife Robyn celebrated their tenth year of marriage in 1990. They have five children, including twin boys. Robyn and Mel call home an 800-acre cattle farm in Australia. Mel is well known for his zany impressions of Hollywood stars; Sylvester Stallone, Marlon Brando and James Cagney are among his favourites. Mel doesn't think much of his worldwide sex symbol image. 'If my wife thinks I'm sexy, it means a lot more to me.'

☆

Artie Shaw and Mickey Rooney tie for the record of the most married men in Hollywood, both having been married eight times. Stan Laurel was also married eight times, but his marriages involved only four women, two of whom he married three times.

☆

1943 saw the Hollywood marriage of the decade; Charlie Chaplin, fifty-four, married Eugene O'Neill's eighteen-year-old daughter Oona. It was generally agreed that the marriage would not last. Months before, Charlie had been sued for child support in a paternity suit brought by Hollywood starlet Joan Barry. Even though blood-tests indicated that Charlie could not be the father, a jury decided that he was. This scandal, on top of his reputed radical politics, finished his American movie career.

☆

Richard Burton was fifty-eight, twenty-one years older than his wife Sally, when he died at their Swiss home. They had been married only thirteen months, having met eighteen months earlier during the making of a TV mini series called 'Wagner'. Richard was the star and Sally a production assistant.

☆

In the movie *The Entertainer* (1960) Joan Plowright played the daughter of Laurence Olivier. In real life they were husband and wife.

☆

Only two Hollywood actresses have married royalty; Rita Hayworth married Prince Aly Khan in 1949, and Grace Kelly married Prince Rainier in 1956.

☆

The voice of the computer in the TV series 'Star Trek' was Majel Barrett, whose husband is Gene Roddenberry, creator/producer of the series.

☆

Lucille Ball's first husband Desi Arnaz was six years her junior. In the smash hit TV series 'I Love Lucy', his age was always older than hers and in real life the age difference was never discussed.

☆

Singer Jane Froman, who survived a plane crash in the early 1940s, later married the pilot who saved her life.

☆

Actress Maureen O'Hara married Charles Blain in March 1968 for the third time. In 1951 Charles became the first man to fly solo over the North Pole in a single-engined aircraft.

☆

English actress Lesley-Ann Down is married to William Friedkind who directed *The Exorcist* and *The French Connection*. As soon as their son Jack was born, Lesley took a year off acting, which meant she lost the female lead in the TV series 'The Thorn Birds'; it went to her good friend Rachel Ward.

☆

In 1963 Eddie Fisher, then Elizabeth Taylor's husband, was paid $1,500 a day to see that his wife got to work on time. She was starring in *Cleopatra* at the time.

☆

William Holden was best man at the wedding of Ronald and Nancy Reagan.

☆

In 1974 Liza Minnelli married Jack Haley Jr. Jack Haley Sr played the Tin Man in *The Wizard of Oz* and escorted Liza's mum, Judy Garland, down the yellow brick road. Liza and Jack divorced in 1978.

☆

The three wives of American TV talk show host Johnny Carson have been named Joan, Joanne and Joanna.

☆

Composer Andrew Lloyd-Webber has been married twice, and both his wives were called Sarah. His second, Sarah Brightman, was a dancer in his London production of *Cats*; he later fell in love with her when he heard her sing Rachmaninov in Russian.

☆

Mickey Rooney's first wife was Ava Gardner.

☆

Singer Pat Boone married the daughter of country and western singer Red Foley.

☆

Greer Garson married Walter Pidgeon in nine movies, but in real life they never tied the knot.

☆

When Elizabeth Taylor married her seventh husband, John Warner, she told the press, 'I don't think of John as husband number seven. He's number one all the way, the best lover I've ever had!'

☆

Wallace Beery was married to Gloria Swanson for only three weeks.

☆

Alfred Hitchcock and his wife were married for fifty-six years, which in Hollywood is quite a record.

☆

In *The Detective* (1968) Frank Sinatra sacked his then wife, actress Mia Farrow, from the movie and replaced her with Jacqueline Bisset.

☆

Actress Joyce Mathews could never quite make up her mind about her husbands. She married Milton Berle in 1941, divorced him in 1947, remarried him in 1949 and divorced him again in 1950. Then she married Billy Rose in 1956, divorced him in 1959, remarried him in 1961 and divorced him in 1963.

☆

Australian actor Paul Hogan and his wife Noelene were divorced in 1981 but remarried six months later. Paul eventually left his wife to marry Linda Kozlowski, his *Crocodile Dundee* co-star.

☆

When Joan Collins was asked about her first marriage to actor Maxwell Reed, she said, 'That ended after twelve months in 1952 when the bastard tried to sell me to a sheik for $20,000.'

☆

Lyricist Alan Jay Lerner was married eight times.

Hollywood's greatest divorce scandal erupted in 1949, when Ingrid Bergman filed for divorce from Dr Peter Lindstrom, having found romance and true love with Italian movie director Roberto Rossellini. At the time her unconventional behaviour, including premarital pregnancy, was headlines all over the world. Today in Hollywood it wouldn't even be noticed.

☆

The largest alimony claim ever filed in Los Angeles was by twenty-three-year-old Sheika Dena, who filed for $3 billion from her twenty-eight-year-old husband, Sheik Mohammed Al-Fassi, for part of the property they had accumulated since their marriage. The court awarded her $81 million, which she settled for. The Sheik is part of the Royal Family of Saudi Arabia.

☆

Every time Joan Crawford changed her husbands, she would cut them out of every picture in the house, then change every toilet seat, and finally even change the name of her house. She did not want anything to remind her of them ever again.

☆

About fifty years ago it was discovered that not all Stan Laurel's comic genius was saved for his movies. Stan's Russian wife Illenana testified in the American divorce court that Stan once dug a grave in their back yard and tried to bury her alive. She went on to say that Stan brought one of his ex-wives along on their honeymoon to reminisce. And yet another ex-Mrs Stan Laurel sent Illenana a congratulatory telegram warning her to get out of the marriage while she could, because Stan was severely unbalanced.

Brief Biographies

Peter Ustinov holds the record when it comes to the file marked 'Done that – been there'. He's written twenty-three plays, nine books and eight movie scripts, acted in thirty-eight movies and twenty stage plays, directed eight movies and eight stage plays and produced ten operas.

☆

Sean Connery has made over fifty movies. In 1988 he won his first Oscar for Best Supporting Actor as cop Jim Malone in *The Untouchables*. He was thirty-two when he became James Bond for the first time; he went on to play 007 in seven movies. In 1969 he made his first James Bond comeback, receiving one million dollars plus 12.5 percent of the profits. Sean hated every minute he had to wear his James Bond toupee, and got rid of it the second he gave up his licence to kill.

☆

French stage actress Sarah Bernhardt had a wooden leg, was an illegitimate child and during her early life slept in a coffin.

☆

Bette Davis worked as a waitress, usher and factory worker before getting her acting break. Five years before her death she came across the time-clock she'd punched every morning as a teenage factory worker and bought it. Now that very clock is at the 20th Century Archive at Boston University, whose Bette Davis Collection holds more than 109,000 items.

☆

George Raft won first prize in a tango contest in the 1920s, and was billed as 'the fastest dancer in the world'. In 1932 he made his movie debut in *Taxi*, as a dancer. In 1937 he turned down the lead in *Dead End*, and in 1941 he turned down both *The Maltese Falcon* and *High Sierra*. Humphrey Bogart played all three parts.

☆

As a child, Debbie Reynolds was an avid Girl Scout of America, winning forty-eight merit badges.

☆

Olivia Newton John was born in Cambridge, England. When she was five, her father moved the family to Australia, where he took up a job as headmaster of a Melbourne grammar school. At the age of fifteen Olivia went back to live in England, and a couple of years later toured with Cliff Richard. She still calls Australia home.

☆

August 24th 1970 and November 24th 1970 are two days that Farrah Fawcett will never forget. She was arrested on both dates for shoplifting, and in both cases pleaded guilty.

☆

Silent screen star Gloria Swanson had a wait of eighteen years between *Nero's Mistress* (1956) and *Airport 75* (1974), where she played herself.

☆

Harrison Ford struggled before reaching the top. After bit parts in such TV shows as 'Gunsmoke', 'Ironside' and 'The Virginian', and a role in the 1970 flop *Zabriskie Point*, he became a carpenter. George Lucas cast Ford in *American Graffiti* in 1972, but Ford didn't hang up his carpenter's tools until the 1976 blockbuster *Star Wars*.

☆

James Caan was a rodeo rider until a talent scout talked him out of riding and into acting. He and Robert De Niro attended the same Manhattan high school, Rhodes High, and later starred together in *The Godfather, Part II* (1974).

☆

At the age of fourteen Jerry Hall announced to her father, a long-distance lorry driver, and her mother, a medical records clerk, 'Ah'm goin' to be real famous and real rich some day.' The 5ft 11in model has lived up to her prediction. She was 'discovered' by a model agent scout on a St Tropez nudist beach in 1972.

☆

Raquel Welch was once crowned Miss San Diego. Her first TV appearances were as a weather girl on a San Diego TV station, a job she took up a few weeks after leaving high school.

☆

In 1973, on his twenty-ninth wedding anniversary, Jerry Lewis went to the bathroom of his Bel Air mansion and put the muzzle of a .38-calibre revolver into his mouth. Then he heard his children laughing in a nearby room, which was the only thing that stopped him from pulling the trigger. Jerry had been driven to the verge of suicide by his long addiction to the painkiller Percodan, which he came to rely on after chipping a bone in his upper spinal column while doing a Las Vegas season in 1965.

While working as a comic in Atlantic City in 1946 he met up with an Italian singer named Dean Martin, and they put together one of the most successful partnerships in American show business. It lasted well into a decade before strong differences busted up the pair in 1959. The annual Jerry Lewis Muscular Dystrophy Telethons have to date drawn well over $600 million in donations, which must be a record amount of money given to an organisation headed by one movie star.

☆

Although Lucille Ball made seventy-four movies and hundreds of TV appearances, she only once appeared on the stage, in a show called *Wildcats* on Broadway in 1960.

☆

Bianca Jagger, born Bianca Perez Morena De Macias, is the youngest person ever to be placed in the Best Dressed Hall of Fame. She once said about her gay friends, 'Homosexuals make the best friends because they care about you as a woman and are not jealous. They love you but don't try to screw up your head.'

☆

Robert Blake, who played 'Baretta' in the TV series for many years, appeared in forty *Our Gang* and *Little Rascals* movies over a five-year period.

☆

In his youth Steve McQueen was caught stealing hubcaps and was sent to reform school.

☆

Ryan O'Neal once spent fifty-one days in jail for punching out the entertainment editor of the *New Orleans Times*. When asked what his most memorable moment in show business was, he replied, 'The greatest moment of my career was on the set of *Barry Lyndon*. After a very difficult take Stanley Kubrick found a way to walk past me, giving instruction to the crew. But as he passed me, he grabbed my hand and squeezed it. It was the most beautiful and appreciated gesture in my life.'

☆

Robert Blake, born Michael Gubitosi, was pushed into his parents' song-and-dance act at the age of two. At seven, Robert played an extra in a couple of *Our Gang* movies.

☆

At the age of eighteen Dudley Moore won an organ scholarship to Magdalen College, Oxford.

☆

Christina Kapsallis Savalas, mother of Telly Savalas, is a former Miss Greece. Telly has a master's degree in psychology, and hosted a talk show on radio in the 1950s called 'Voice of America'.

☆

Coming up to forty with five children to bring up, Phyllis Diller was a copywriter for a California radio station before she found fame and fortune as a stand-up comic at the Purple Onion nightclub in San Francisco in 1955. In the 60s she was named one of the world's most outrageous stars for remarks like – 'When I go to the beach wearing a bikini, even the tide won't come in!' Her idol and good friend is Bob Hope.

☆

In the 1960s Bette Midler, still a struggling actress, worked her way up from the chorus to a leading role as Tevye's eldest daughter in the Broadway show *Fiddler on the Roof*.

☆

Actor Mark Harmon once taught a class on option geometry at West Point. In the mid-eighties he was named the world's sexiest man.

☆

Greta Garbo turned down $25,000 for a single guest appearance on radio in 1934. She never spoke on radio, in fact she did not like the idea of radio at all.

☆

Joan Collins's first job in theatre was assistant stage manager in Maidstone, Kent. She swept the stage, helped to prompt the actors and was the dresser for the leading lady. At nineteen she signed up with the J. Arthur Rank Organization for $120 a week. Not until well into her forties, however, when she played Blake Carrington's wife in 'Dynasty' did she suddenly become a superstar. In 1983, at the age of fifty, she posed seminude for *Playboy* magazine, which made the issue a complete sellout. In 1985 America's *TV Guide* magazine named her the most beautiful woman on TV.

☆

George C. Scott had a tumulous and very unhappy childhood in Michigan; his mother died when he was eight and his father ruled the house with an iron fist. In 1971 George starred in *Patton*, for which he won an Academy Award, which he turned down. He was married twice to actress Colleen Dewhurst.

☆

Jim Henson met his wife Jane in a puppetry class at the University of Maryland. Soon after, they landed a five-minute late night puppet show on local TV called 'Sam and Friends.' The star of that series, in 1956, was Kermit the Frog, a rather articulate amphibian made out of green curtain material with a couple of ping-pong balls for eyes.

☆

From 1954 to 1957 Tommy Rettig played Jeff Miller in the TV series 'Lassie'. He was a major child star in the 1950s; at the age of five he starred with Mary Martin in the stage show *Annie Get Your Gun*. In 1975 he was sentenced to five years in prison for smuggling cocaine.

☆

When rock queen Tina Turner turned the big five-0 in 1989, she hired London's ultra-exclusive Reform Club and had it decorated with hundreds of white lillies and over 1,000 white candles. Her birthday cake stood three feet high, was topped with a life-size royal crown, and cost a whopping $8,000. Tina arrived in a Dior one-off designer gown at a cost of $40,000. Her guests included Shirley Bassey, Dire Straits, Duran Duran, Jerry Hall, Mick Jagger and Eric Clapton. In her birthday speech Tina said she did not worry about turning fifty, in fact she hasn't worried about age since she became a Buddhist.

☆

A broom closet at the Hollywood Roosevelt was home to a penniless undiscovered actor called David Niven. 'When I first arrived in California, broke and twenty-two years old, I had no training as an actor. Al Weingard was then the reception clerk at the Roosevelt Hotel. I met him and he gave me a room in the servants' quarters.'

Cary Grant was a great Cole Porter fan, and in 1945 he played Cole Porter in the movie *Night And Day*.

When Humphrey Bogart was a baby, his mother entered him in a competition to find the Mellin's Baby Food ideal baby. Humphrey won, and his baby picture was used in the company's advertising.

Peter Tork, one of the original Monkees, was sent to a federal prison in 1972 for possession of marijuana.

Lana Turner was discovered at the Top Hat Malt Shop in Hollywood, not at Schwab's Drugstore.

At the tender age of seven George Burns joined the Pee Wee Choir, to raise money. The choir would stand on New York street corners singing for money.

Betty Grable and Veronica Lake were good friends; they were also two of Hollywood's most famous pin-up stars in the 1940s. In July 1973 they died within five days of each other.

☆

When Angela Lansbury played Laurence Harvey's mother in *The Manchurian Candidate*, she was in fact only three years older than him.

☆

In 1930 a young model was crowned Miss New Orleans. Part of her prize was a Hollywood screen test. Her name was Dorothy Lamour. She and an unknown called Clark Gable started work on the same day in Hollywood.

☆

The strangest movie executive even by Hollywood standards was Mack Sennett of Keystone Cops fame. The only way he could relax was in hot water, where he said he got his best inspirations for his comedies. Mack even had a bathtub installed in the centre of his Hollywood office.

☆

Mae West appeared on stage in 1926 in a play she both wrote and produced called *Sex*. During the second half of the show the New York police raided the theatre, and Miss West was found guilty of public obscenity. She was sentenced to ten days' jail on Welfare Island, and fined $500. Eight days later she was released, with two days off for good behaviour.

☆

Noel Coward was a grammar school drop-out.

In the 1960s Sean Connery emerged a star, and not just as James Bond. He beat Elvis Presley and the Beatles in British box-office polls; publicists reckon that in the 60s his face sold more magazines than any other star, including America's then First Lady, Jackie Kennedy.

Margaret Hamilton, who played the Wicked Witch of the West in *The Wizard of Oz* (1939), was the founder of a kindergarten in the Presbyterian church in Beverly Hills. She also served as president of the Beverly Hills Board of Education for several years. She died on 16th May 1985.

For a brief period in the early 1950s actress June Haver became a nun, then left and married actor Fred MacMurray.

☆

In 1951 a young Larry Hagman accompanied his mother Mary Martin to London, where she starred in the stage show *South Pacific* at Drury Lane. Larry got himself into the show as an extra for just $24 a week. After the show ended he stayed on in Europe and served with the United States Air Force. He married the love of his life, Maj, a Swedish dress designer, in 1954.

June Havoc is the younger sister of Gypsy Rose Lee and was once billed as Dainty Baby Jane in a vaudeville act. She married at thirteen and was a mother at sixteen. She once danced in a marathon which lasted for four months. She and her partner came second, winning $100 for some 3,000 hours of dancing.

☆

At just fifteen, Richard Burton won his first prize fight. A few years later he won a scholarship to Exeter College, Oxford. Later he was offered an appointment as a don at the university, but turned it down.

☆

Michael Caine had to redub his lines 127 times for *Alfie*, to make his accent intelligible for American audiences.

☆

Tom Cruise suffered from dyslexia, as did both his mother and sister. As a child he was put on a special reading course.

☆

Elizabeth Taylor was brought up as a Christian Scientist. She turned to the Jewish faith when she married Eddie Fisher.

☆

Valerie Harper is one of the founders of LIFE – which stands for 'Love Is Feeding Everyone' – an organisation to feed the hungry people of Los Angeles.

☆

Walter Matthau was six feet tall at the age of eleven. He used to play with a neighbourhood friend called Rocky Graziano, whom Walter says he used to beat up every now and then.

☆

Roger Moore played the 'Saint' on TV for six and a half years. The son of a London policeman, Roger was fired from his first job for pocketing the expenses money.

☆

Because of his involvement in liberal causes in 1972, Paul Newman appeared on President Richard Nixon's original list of twenty enemies. He was the only actor listed.

☆

On 8th April 1986 Clint Eastwood won a landslide victory to be elected Mayor of Carmel, California, with the largest voter turnout in the town's history. His first act as Mayor was to legalize ice-cream parlours in Carmel.

☆

In 1927 a teenager named Ginger Rogers was placed first in a Texas statewide Charleston contest. The trophy was presented by actor Dick Powell, who told the eager teenager she should try acting and go to Hollywood.

☆

Steve Martin was a cheerleader at high school in Texas where he was born.

☆

Before he became a full-time singer Art Garfunkel majored in architecture at Columbia University in New York.

☆

Beautiful actress Kim Basinger was once an agoraphobic who didn't want to leave her house for months at a time.

☆

Rosco 'Fatty' Arbuckle was the first American actor to endorse advertising for cigarettes. In the 1920s Fatty Arbuckle was the centre of an enormous scandal, standing trial for the rape and murder of a young actress called Virginia Rappe. After the scandal he went on to direct movies under the name of William Goodrich. Silent comedy star Buster Keaton suggested that Fatty call himself Will B. Good instead of William Goodrich.

☆

At the age of twelve singer/actress Olivia Newton John won an English Hayley Mills look-alike contest.

☆

In 1949 Robert Mitchum was up on a charge of possessing marijuana. He asked the judge for a delay in his sentencing so that he could finish filming *The Big Steal*.

☆

Superstar Mel Gibson almost became a Catholic priest instead of a box-office idol. His staunchly religious dad Hutton pounded the faith into all his eleven children. Mel is even named after an Irish Saint. When he was an altar boy, 'I used to trip over my cassock or set myself on fire' he said. At the age of twelve he entered a strict all-boys Catholic school, and began to think about becoming a priest.

☆

George Segal started performing magic tricks at the age of four. When he was twelve he was playing a trombone in the school band.

☆

Rod McKuen got his showbiz start in 1954 at San Francisco's Purple Onion club, under the watchful eye of comic Phyllis Diller. At the club he would sing his own songs and read his own poetry. At one time Rod worked as a blood salesman for a large company, sometimes selling his own blood for $5 a pint. During his childhood he travelled all over America with his dance-hall hostess mother, never knowing his father. At the age of twelve he started to look through every town's phone book for the name McKuen, hoping to find him. In 1976, at the age of forty-three, Rod found the grave of his father, Rodney Marion McKuen, who had died in 1963. The long search is chronicled in his book, *Finding My Father: One Man's Search For Identity*. Rod also sired a son out of wedlock, who lives with his mother in France.

☆

Robert Redford refuses to give autographs, and hates being stopped or pointed out by people in the streets.

☆

Beautiful actress and one time Revlon model Lauren Hutton used to raise earthworms as a child and sell them.

☆

James Mason has a degree in architecture from Cambridge University.

☆

Diahann Carroll, daughter of a Harlem subway conductor, wanted a show-business career from a very early age. She was the very first black actress to star in an American prime-time TV sitcom, 'Julia' (1968).

☆

Charlie Chaplin was officially banned from the USA in the early 1950s because of his political beliefs, but in 1972 he returned to Los Angeles to receive a special Academy Award. Charlie's last movie appearance was in *A Countess from Hong Kong* (1967), which he wrote and directed, starring Sophia Loren and Marlon Brando. He played a cameo role of a seasick steward.

☆

The FBI held a file on Frank Sinatra. It weighed fourteen pounds.

☆

In 1935 Lucille Ball was playing movie extra parts at RKO Studios. The studio thought she would never amount to much as an actress so they fired her. A few years later she bought the studio and fired the boss who fired her.

☆

On 18th May 1989 actor Rob Lowe was caught in a compromising position by Fulton County officials who announced they had a home video of night games starring Rob and an underage girl.

☆

Gummo Marx, an early member of the Marx Brothers, never appeared before the cameras. He quit the act in the early 1920s to become the team's agent and business manager.

☆

Here are some stars who have traded their glitzy designer outfits for jailbird stripes; Sophia Loren, seventeen days for tax evasion; George C. Scott, one night for drunk and disorderly; Stacy Keach, six months for cocaine smuggling; Jane Russell, four days for drunk driving; Chuck Berry, 120 days for tax evasion; Richard Pryor, ten days for failing to file an American federal income tax return; Burt Reynolds, a week on a chain gang for vagrancy; Steve McQueen, twenty-one days for going AWOL.

☆

Comedian and TV star Bill Cosby has a PhD in education from the University of Massachusetts.

☆

During World War II, actress Paulette Goddard became the first civilian woman to fly over the Himalaya Mountains.

☆

Maurice Chevalier learned to speak English while held in a German prison camp.

☆

Elizabeth Taylor, Marilyn Monroe and Carroll Baker all converted to Judaism some time during their lives.

☆

When actress/comedian Cloris Leachman was asked by a reporter if that was her real name, she replied, 'Of course it's my real name. Would anyone in their right mind ever change to Cloris Leachman?' At the age of eleven, and with her parents' blessing, Cloris hitchhiked from her home in Des Moines to nearby Drake University, where she won her very first role in a children's radio show. During her long show-business career she even played a brief few episodes on TV as Lassie's owner, but stardom arrived at the age of forty-six when she won an Oscar for her role in *The Last Picture Show* (1972).

Sports, Games and Hobbies of the Stars

Katharine Hepburn won a figure-skating bronze medal in the championships at New York's Madison Square Gardens when she was fourteen years old. At just sixteen she won a Connecticut State gold championship.

Humphrey Bogart had a great passion for chess. He played it on the set, by telephone, and even had it written into the opening scene of *Casablanca*.

Funny lady Phyllis Diller is a very good painter of stylized heads, her work selling for big bucks in art galleries. This is something she has taken up only over the last few years as a hobby.

The 1964 Athlete of the Year in America was Jim Brown, a pro footballer. Soon after, he left the world of sport and became an actor.

☆

When Ted Danson landed the role of bartender Sam Malone on 'Cheers', he went to the American Bartender School and graduated second in his class. Originally his character was meant to be an ex-football player, but at the last minute the show's creators made him an ex-baseball player, because they didn't think Ted looked athletic enough to have played football.

☆

Academy Award winner Robert Duvall was voted by *Tennis* magazine as the best celebrity tennis player.

☆

Actor Eddie Albert is a very keen gardener. He grows corn in the front garden of his Pacific Palisades home and runs a $12,000 air-cooled greenhouse in the back garden where he grows twenty different vegetables.

☆

Zeppo Marx (one of the Marx Brothers) was granted a US patent for a wristwatch that could also check a person's heartbeat.

☆

John Wayne was an excellent card player. He once won Lassie from its owner in a poker game.

☆

Robert Stack was the national 20-gauge rifle champion in 1937, and once held the world's record of 354 consecutive hits.

☆

John Forsyth and his actress wife Julie Warren have been married for forty-two years, which is quite something in Hollywood. Before becoming an actor John was a baseball radio announcer. In 1979 he had quadruple bypass surgery. His first love is horseracing; he owns sixteen horses, and one of his mares has won him well over a quarter of a million dollars. John also breeds horses, and once said he would gladly give up an Academy Award to see one of his horses win the Kentucky Derby.

Lee Majors was orphaned before he was two years old. At high school in his home town in eastern Kentucky he landed a football scholarship, and had his nose broken five times. Lee's first big Hollywood break was playing the bastard son in *The Big Valley*, which starred Barbara Stanwyck. They were firm friends till her death.

Today actor Charlton Heston has another string to his bow; he has been recognized as a talented pen-and-ink artist. Some of his drawings have been exhibited in art galleries around the world.

Johnny Weissmuller was the sixth actor to play Tarzan; the first to play him in the talkies, then in twelve other movies. In 1922, he became the first man to break 1 minute in the 100 metres (58.6 seconds).

☆

Movie mogul Darryl F. Zanuck is in the American Croquet Hall of Fame.

☆

Rossano Brazzi, who starred in *South Pacific*, was once the featherweight boxing champion of Italy, long before he became an actor.

☆

Omar Sharif represented Egypt in the 1964 Olympic Bridge tournament.

☆

Kung Fu movie star king Bruce Lee was cha cha dance champion of Hong Kong in 1958.

☆

Zaca was the only real love of swashbuckling Errol Flynn's life; she was a 36-metre schooner. He and his Hollywood mates had quite a few well-publicized parties on board.

There was a court case brought by a woman who alleged that Errol had sexually assaulted her in the bath aboard *Zaca*; Errol won. A matter of weeks after his marriage to his third wife, Patrice Wymore, Errol was handed a writ aboard *Zaca*, claiming he had raped a seventeen-year-old girl the year before. In court Errol claimed that he had never set eyes on the girl, and told the judge it was a set-up, adding, 'Anyway, I could never make love to a girl with hairy legs.' The judge believed him, and the case was thrown out of court.

☆

Actor Cornel Wilde was such a good fencer that he was selected for the American team for the 1936 Olympics, held in Berlin. He declined for personal reasons.

☆

Christopher Reeve, star of *Superman* movies, is a pilot, and operates a fleet of cargo planes based in Peterboro, New Jersey.

☆

In 1932 Alan Ladd was an American diving champion, and also held a 50-yards freestyle record. Years later he was a lifeguard at North Hollywood Park, where Lee Majors was also a lifeguard in his teen years.

☆

The largest yacht ever owned by a star is *Principia*, a classic 90-foot motor yacht owned by singer John Davidson.

☆

As a boy, Alec Guinness was a short-distance runner, and the holder of many awards.

☆

Peter Sellers's interest in judo earned him the title of vice president of the London Judo Society.

☆

Tasmanian born Errol Flynn was expelled from school three times. The only thing he excelled at there was tennis.

☆

In his youth, French actor Jean-Paul Belmondo was an amateur boxer.

☆

Noel Harrison, Rex Harrison's son, was in the British Olympic ski team in 1952 and 1956.

☆

Kenny Rogers has a 1,200-acre farm in Georgia, where he breeds Arab horses and cattle.

☆

Buster Crabbe, who starred in *Flash.Gordon* as well as in a string of B-grade movies, won the 400 metres freestyle gold medal for swimming when he represented America at the 1932 Olympic Games.

☆

In 1970 Ryan O'Neal won the Los Angeles Silver Annual Handball Tournament. He has also been a contestant in the West Coast Golden Gloves competition.

☆

Paramount Studios' biggest star of the 1920s was Clara Bow, the 'It' girl, one of Hollywood's first sex symbols. She once claimed to have slept with the entire University of Southern California football team. When the news hit the headlines, the studio raised her salary by $5,000 a week and made her into an even bigger star.

In Which They Served:
MILITARY AND OTHER CONNECTIONS

Major Clark Gable's American discharge papers were signed in June 1944, by Captain Ronald Reagan.

☆

America's Sweetheart, Mary Pickford, was made an honorary US Army Colonel during World War I. In 1908 she made her acting debut in a play called *The Warrens Of Virginia*, written by William De Mille, the brother of Cecil B. Mary kept a specially bound copy of that play on her office desk until the day she died.

☆

Kris Kristofferson was a helicopter pilot in the American Army.

☆

Cliff Robertson's ship was bombed in the Pacific shortly after Pearl Harbor, and Merchant Marine Cliff Robertson was reported among the dead. Months later he turned up alive and healthy in La Jolla, California. Years later he portrayed a similar World War II survivor, John F. Kennedy, in *PT 109*. Today Cliff is an avid flyer and owns six vintage airplanes.

☆

In 1942 the Armed Forces American Radio Network was started by GIs in Alaska, who built a radio station to fill in time, then wrote to every leading Hollywood star asking them to record messages. Within a year, there were 306 stations in forty-seven countries. Not one Hollywood star ever turned down a request from the Armed Forces Radio Network.

☆

Before he became an actor, Ernest Borgnine spent ten years in the US Navy. His first big TV role was starring in 'McHale's Navy', where his navy background was put to good use.

☆

Anthony Quayle served with the Royal Artillery, and held the rank of Major during World War II. He was sent on several secret missions for both the Americans and British.

☆

Both Ernest Hemingway and Walt Disney served as ambulance drivers in and after World War I. They then teamed up at the *Kansas City Star*, Walt as an artist and Ernest as a reporter.

☆

In 1964 silent movie star Bebe Daniels was given the Presidential Medal of Freedom for her efforts in entertaining American servicemen overseas during World War II. She was also the first female civilian to enter Normandy after the D-day invasion.

☆

Actor Ted Knight won five Bronze Stars in World War II.

☆

Actor Glen Ford is a captain in the US Naval Reserves. In the mid-1960s he served in Vietnam as commander of a Marine battalion, and was shot down twice in a helicopter. His uncle, Sir John MacDonald, was a former prime minister of Canada.

☆

Al Jolson was the first American entertainer to entertain the troops in Korea. He was sent by the United Nations.

☆

Gene Autry, one of Hollywood's first superstar cowboys, was a cargo pilot during World War II.

☆

Errol Flynn wrote in his autobiography, *My Wicked, Wicked Ways*, that he fought alongside Fidel Castro and his forces in Cuba in 1959.

☆

Jimmy Stewart retired with the rank of Brigadier General in 1968, after twenty-seven years in the Air Force reserve. He was awarded the American Distinguished Service Medal, only the second time that this award had been bestowed on a reserve officer. Jimmy is very proud of the twenty combat missions he flew during World War II.

☆

America's most decorated war hero in World War II was Audie Murphy. After lying about his age to join the army at just seventeen, he was wounded three times and credited with killing 240 Germans. Audie and a friend were the only two to survive out of a company of 235 men. Before he turned twenty-one he had won twenty-seven medals, including three from the French and one from Belgium. In 1955 he starred in a movie version of his autobiography *To Hell and Back*, which started him on an acting career. He died in 1971 at the age of forty-seven and is buried in the Arlington National Cemetery.

Family Ties

Charles Bronson said in an interview that his family was so poor that he started school in dresses which were hand-me-downs from his older sister.

Zany actress Carol Channing's father, George, was editor-in-chief of the Christian Science magazine and head lecturer for the organization in San Francisco.

Lucille Ball's first husband Desi Arnaz's father and great-grandfather were both Mayors of Santiago in Cuba. Desi's father, elected at twenty-nine, is still the youngest Mayor Santiago has ever had.

Clara Bow was a very bad insomniac after her mother tried to stab her.

Dirk Bogarde's father was once editor of *The Times*.

Top model Cheryl Tieg's father is an undertaker in California.

☆

Hollywood loves royalty, and has tried to cash in on Princess Diana by raking up some of her long-lost relations. Humphrey Bogart is her seventh cousin twice removed, Olivia de Havilland is her fifth cousin three times removed, Orson Welles was her eighth cousin twice removed, Lee Remick is her tenth cousin, and Lillian Gish her double seventh cousin three times removed.

☆

John Barrymore was seduced by his stepmother at the age of fifteen.

☆

Both James Arness and Montgomery Clift had twin sisters.

☆

In 1988 Kris Kristofferson and his wife Lisa became guardians of the three surviving daughters of their housekeeper, Maria Juana Aguilar, who begged the Kristoffersons to look out for her children a week before she was shot to death by her common-law husband. The judge awarded the couple total custody of Maris, 4, Marta, 9, and Brenda, 12.

☆

Ginger Rogers's real mother Lela played her screen mother in *The Major and the Minor* (1942).

☆

Burt Reynolds's father was once the Chief of Police in Rivera Beach, Florida.

☆

Kirk Douglas, born Issur Danielovitch Demsky, grew up the only boy among six girls. His parents were impoverished Russian immigrants in Amsterdam, New York.

☆

A few days after she turned one year old, Brooke Shields was a professional model. At twelve she played a child prostitute in the controversial *Pretty Baby*, which attracted international attention. Brooke's mother Teri is the driving force behind the scenes. Brooke was born four months after Teri's marriage to Frank Shields, who was vice-president of the cosmetic empire of Helena Rubinstein. Their marriage lasted only a matter of weeks.

☆

Lon Chaney's parents were deaf mutes.

☆

Director Blake Edwards's grandfather, J. Gordon Edwards, directed silent screen star Theda Bara in more than twenty of her films.

☆

Alan Whicker was born in Cairo, and is an only child. His father was an army officer who died when Alan was four years old.

☆

In 1950 actress Jane Fonda was told that her mother Frances had died of a heart attack. A year later Jane found out that she had in fact committed suicide, when she read an article in a Hollywood gossip magazine.

☆

Actor Ben Kingsley's father was an Indian doctor who lived in Manchester. His mother Anna was an English fashion model.

☆

Robert Wagner was the only son of a wealthy Detroit metal manufacturer. At school he was a real rebel, being expelled from several fashionable prep schools. He worked at Warner Bros. as an extra in over forty movies, until Spencer Tracy took him under his wing in the 1950s.

☆

Clint Eastwood cut his teeth on a TV series called 'Rawhide' playing Rowdy Yates from 1959 to 1966. Clint is believed to be a direct descendant of John Eastwood, Sheriff and Mayor of Dublin in 1679. The seventeenth-century lawman was a refined and wealthy nobleman granted his personal coat of arms in 1658. The crest, depicting a wild boar – the heraldic symbol of power – now hangs in Clint's home in Carmel, California.

☆

Tyrone Power and his father both appeared in a Chicago stage production of *The Merchant of Venice*.

☆

Pamela Stevenson was born in Auckland, New Zealand. Both her parents are doctors who are involved in cancer research. She is a teetotaller, non-smoker and a vegetarian.

☆

In 1950 Marilyn Monroe starred in *The Asphalt Jungle*. Also up for the lead was Georgia Holt, better known today as Cher's mother.

☆

Some Hollywood movies have kept it all in the family. In *The Ten Commandments* (1956) the infant Moses was played by Fraser Heston, while his dad Charlton played Moses. *Doctor Zhivago*, starring Omar Sharif as Yuri Zhivago, had his son Tarek play Zhivago at the age of seven. In a TV movie, 'Moses' (1975), Will Lancaster played a young Moses while his father Burt played the adult.

☆

Tallulah Bankhead's father was Speaker in the House of Representatives.

☆

Actress Kristy McNichol's parents were divorced when she was three. Kristy's movie-extra mother got her quite a few starring roles in TV commercials by the time she was eight. At twelve she landed the role of Buddy on the smash hit TV series 'Family' and at fifteen she won a TV Emmy for her role in the show.

☆

Erich Segal, who wrote the novel *Love Story* on which the movie was based, was the son of a rabbi.

☆

Max Born, Nobel Prize-winning German physicist, was grandfather to Olivia Newton John.

☆

Actor Billy De Williams has a twin sister.

☆

The fathers of David Frost, Alistair Cooke and Laurence Olivier were all in the ministry.

☆

Red Skelton's father was a circus clown, which gave Red his interest in painting clowns – now a very much sought after item by art collectors around the world.

☆

Oliver Reed is the nephew of movie director Sir Carol Reed. Whenever there is a royal birthday, he flies two large Union Jacks from the roof of his Sussex farmhouse.

☆

Margaux and Mariel Hemingway are the granddaughters of Ernest Hemingway.

☆

Bill Cosby's children are named Erika, Erinn, Ensa, Camille, Evin and Ennis.

☆

Sylvester Stallone's father played the timekeeper in the first *Rocky* movie.

☆

Jaclyn Smith's grandfather lived to be 102 years old. She says one of her ambitions is to do the same.

☆

When Tatum O'Neal was three years old her father Ryan, then starring in the TV soap 'Peyton Place' divorced her mother Joanna Moore. On the same day he married 'Peyton Place' co-star Leigh Taylor-Young. Ryan lost custody of Tatum to her mother. At the age of eight she ran away to her father. The resulting custody battle featured high courtroom dramas of drug addiction and child abuse, supposed to have occurred while Tatum and her younger brother Griffin lived with her mother in a wild hippie commune.

☆

Rita Hayworth is the first cousin of Ginger Rogers; their mothers were sisters.

☆

Actress Sally Field's stepfather, Jock Mahoney, played Tarzan in the early 1960s.

☆

During the Franco-Prussian War Marlene Dietrich's father, Louis Dietrich, was awarded the Iron Cross. He was a cavalry major.

☆

Warren Beatty is the real-life brother of Shirley MacLaine.

☆

Here are a few celebrities whose dads were in the US military: Kris Kristofferson – US Air Force General; John Denver – US Air Force Lieutenant-Colonel; Victoria Principal – US Air Force Master Sergeant; Steve McQueen – US Navy pilot; Jim Morrison – US Navy Admiral; Priscilla Presley – US Navy pilot; stepfather US Air Force Major; Faye Dunaway – US Army Sergeant; James Woods – US Army Major.

☆

Sophia Loren's sister Maria married the son of the Italian dictator Benito Mussolini.

☆

George Burns came from a family of seven sisters and four brothers.

☆

Carol Burnett's parents, both alcoholics, abandoned her to be raised by her grandmother Mae, a powerhouse of a Christian Scientist church. It was Mae to whom Carol would later signal on TV every week by tugging at her right earlobe, sending her a good night message.

☆

Marlon Brando's mother was the person who encouraged Henry Fonda to become an actor. She talked him into trying for a part at a local playhouse.

☆

Anne Baxter's grandfather was a highly respected American architect Frank Lloyd Wright.

☆

Country and Western singer Loretta Lynn was married at the age of fifteen, and became a grandmother at twenty-nine. Her sister is singer Crystal Gayle, whose real name is Brenda. The nickname comes from the Krystal hamburger chain in Kentucky where she was born.

☆

At the taping of a 'Lucy Special' in 1978, Lucille Ball made her first entrance down a flight of stairs and the studio audience went wild with applause. As her feet hit the third step she burst into tears and the taping had to be stopped. She stepped out of the madcap Lucy character to speak to her loving audience, telling them that it was the first time she had taped a show since her mother's death and it hit her very hard, realizing that DeDe, her mother, was not in the studio audience. A few moments later she pulled herself together and went on with the show as if nothing had happened. That day in 1978 was the last time Lucy and Vivian Vance ever worked together; six months later Vivian died of cancer.

☆

Mickey Rooney's son, Mickey Jr., was one of the original members of the 'Mouseketeers' on the American TV show 'The Mickey Mouse Club'.

☆

Elvis Presley was very close to his parents, and in *Loving You* (1957) he had them appear as extras. It was their first and last movie.

☆

The sons of Paul Newman, Dan Dailey, Gregory Peck and Mary Tyler Moore, all committed suicide.

☆

Cher's mother Georgia Holt has been married eight times, thrice to the same man. Cher still feels very bitter towards her father who abandoned her in 1945 when she was only one year old.

☆

The sons of Marlon Brando and Frank Sinatra have both been kidnapped and later returned to their fathers, Christian Brando in 1972 and Frank Sinatra Jr. in 1964.

☆

Jane Wyman's double in *Stage Fright* (1950) was Alfred Hitchcock's daughter Patricia.

☆

In 1950 at the age of ten, Peter Fonda shot himself in the kidneys and liver when he found out his mother Frances had committed suicide.

☆

As a child, actor Tony Randall attended twenty-four schools, because his father was always on the road selling art in the Palm Beach and New York areas.

☆

There are quite a few stars in Hollywood who are related, but perform under different surnames. Katherine Houghton is the niece of Katharine Hepburn; Jamie Lee Curtis is the daughter of Janet Leigh and Tony Curtis; Larry Hagman is the son of Mary Martin; James MacArthur is the son of Helen Hayes; Joely Richardson is the daughter of Vanessa Redgrave; Carrie Fisher is the daughter of Debbie Reynolds and Eddie Fisher; Mia Farrow is the daughter of Maureen O'Sullivan; Emilio Estevez and Charlie Sheen are sons of Martin Sheen.

Sam Marx, the father of the Marx Brothers, always wanted to be an actor, so in *Monkey Business* (1931) Sam appeared as an extra.

☆

Sylvester Stallone's son is named Sage Moonblood.

☆

James Stewart's son was killed while serving in Vietnam in 1969.

Controversial TV actor Ed Asner is the son of a Kansas City scrap-iron dealer.

Jocelyn Brando appeared alongside her brother Marlon in *The Ugly American* (1963).

☆

Grace Kelly's father, John Brendan Kelly, was the National Physical Fitness Director under President Herbert Hoover. He also won a gold medal in the 1920 Olympics in Antwerp in scull-racing, singles and doubles. Her mother, Margaret Majer, was a champion swimmer.

☆

Nancy Reagan is the daughter of a New Jersey car salesman.

☆

In 1940 *Life* magazine called Bing Crosby 'Hollywood's Proudest Father'. That image was totally shattered in 1983 when, six years after Bing's death, his son Gary published a tell-all book portraying his father as a cold disciplinarian who ridiculed his four sons and beat Gary until he drew blood.

Home Sweet Home

When Joan Crawford bought a new house, the first thing she did was to remove all the bathtubs. She said it was totally unsanitary to sit in one's dirty bathwater.

☆

Jean Harlow bought her first house in 1931 at 9820 Easton Drive, Beverly Hills. At the end of each rain gutter spout she had the builder place hand-carved, head-sized wooden likenesses of her friends Rudolph Valentino, Douglas Fairbanks Sr. and Mary Pickford.

☆

Robert Vaughn and his family live in a three-storey classic twenty-three-room mansion in Ridgefield, Connecticut, which was built in 1905 by the Houdini family.

☆

The first swimming pool ever built in the Los Angeles area was at the famous home of Mary Pickford and Douglas Fairbanks. The pool was so large that Mary and Douglas could go canoeing in it. The pool is still at 'Pickfair'.

☆

Sammy Davis Jr. and his wife Altovise had a real talking-point at the bottom of their Beverly Hills garden. It was an ape-man statue that dominated everything. It came from *Planet of the Apes* (1968), a gift to the Davises from the producer, Arthur Jacobs. It was given as a joke, but they liked it so much they had their entire garden redesigned to feature the twelve-foot-high white statue.

☆

Lucille Ball's house in Beverley Hills is the house most tourists want to see in Los Angeles, according to Hollywood tour guides.

☆

The second most popular home of a Hollywood star is that of Robert Wagner and his late wife Natalie Wood. The interest arises from Natalie's bizarre death by drowning from their yacht in the early 1980s.

☆

Mae West hated the colour of the building her apartment looked out on. She asked the owners to change it on more than one occasion, but they always refused, so she bought it and immediately had it painted her favourite shade – white.

☆

Judy Garland holds the record for the movie star who has lived in the most houses. In Hollywood alone she is thought to have lived in more than twenty-five, and she had other homes outside LA.

☆

Burt Reynolds owns a 170-acre ranch in Jupiter, Florida, which was built in the 1920s by gangster Al Capone. When Burt built the Burt Reynolds Dinner Theatre in Florida he had his own VIP box built, and nobody is allowed to sit in it unless they are with Burt. When he is not there, it is kept firmly shut.

☆

When Jermaine Jackson – one of Michael's brothers – bought his 1.9 acre mansion estate (once the home of Johnny Wiessmuller) he decided to have gates built to give him and his family more privacy. These became the most expensive gates ever to adorn a private home in Beverly Hills, costing a quarter of a million dollars and personalized with initialled crests. The sixteen-foot-high gates were considered an eyesore by Jermaine's wealthy neighbours, who instantly demanded he take them down. Only weeks after they were installed, he was ordered to have them cut in half to conform with the local zoning.

☆

Mae West holds the record for a Hollywood star living the longest in the same apartment. She lived in the Ravenswood apartment block from 1932 until she died in 1980. Her apartment was totally white-on-white. Even today her penthouse is pointed out on just about every Hollywood tour. For many years it was thought that she owned the whole block of apartments, but after her death it was found that she only owned her own.

☆

The 1976 singer Engelbert Humperdinck bought the Holmby Hills Los Angeles home of the late Jayne Mansfield, which was painted shocking pink and known as The Pink Palace. The house was three-storeyed, Spanish-style, with an elevator and seven fireplaces. Engelbert bought it from a spinster who lived mainly in a back room of the nearly 10,000-square-foot house. It was built in the 1930s for a Texan oilman who sold it to Hollywood star Rudy Vallee, but it only became famous when Jayne bought it and painted it shocking pink. She lived there until she was killed in a car accident in 1967. Jayne and her husband, muscleman Mickey Hargitay, designed and built a heart-shaped swimming pool for their back garden. Mickey wrote 'I love you Jaynie' on the bottom of the pool, which is there to this day. Jayne's initials remain in the wrought-iron gates which face on to Sunset Boulevard. Somewhere in the house there is supposed to be a hidden wall with Jayne's magazine covers, which had all been framed, but nobody has ever found that secret wall.

These are not the only reminders of Jayne to remain in the house. Both Engelbert and his wife have seen her ghost on several occasions.

Debuts

At the 1935 Royal Command Performance, a little three-year-old stepped on to the stage to entertain King George V and Queen Mary, dancing with her ballet class. Her name was Elizabeth Taylor.

☆

Mae West made her first movie at the age of forty.

☆

Spencer Tracy's movie debut was in *Up The River* (1930) with Humphrey Bogart.

☆

Sidney Poitier made his movie debut in the feature thriller *No Way Out* (1950). Many people think his debut was in *The Blackboard Jungle* (1955), but this was his fifth movie.

☆

When Paul Newman saw his first movie, *The Silver Chalice* (1954), he was appalled at his acting. He thought it was so bad that he took out an advertisement in a Los Angeles paper to apologize for what he believed was a poor performance.

☆

Alfred Hitchcock directed Shirley MacLaine in her first movie.

☆

Marilyn Monroe made her film debut as an extra in *Scudda Hoo – Scudda Hay* (1948).

☆

Jon Voight made his Broadway debut in *The Sound of Music*.

☆

Alyssa Milano, the young star of TV's 'Who's the Boss', got her first big break as Annie in the American stage show. She won the role at an open audition of more than 1,000 hopeful little girls.

☆

Woody Allen made his movie debut in *What's New, Pussycat* (1965).

☆

Shelley Winters gave Robert De Niro his first big movie break, playing her son in *Bloody Mama* (1970).

☆

TV actor John Gabriel made his movie debut in *The Young Lions*, playing a corpse.

☆

Robert Mitchum made his debut playing Hopalong Cassidy in the 1943 Western.

☆

The multi-talented daughter of Judy Garland and Vincente Minnelli, Liza Minnelli, was still an infant when she made her movie debut. She was carried in her mother's arms into the happy ending of the musical *In the Good Old Summer Time* (1946).

☆

William Holden's first movie was *Golden Boy* (1939).

☆

Both Charles Bronson and Lee Marvin debuted in *You're in the Navy Now* (1951).

☆

Spencer Tracy started his acting career in 1922 by playing a robot in a Broadway show called *Are You There*.

☆

Actress Geraldine Chaplin made her film debut in her father's movie *Limelight* (1952).

☆

Non-Jewish actor Steve McQueen made his stage debut in a Yiddish-language play.

☆

The American soap 'Dark Shadows' gave ex-'Charlie's Angels' Kate Jackson her first TV role, as a ghost named Daphne Harridge.

☆

Love is on the Air was released in 1937, giving the world a new actor called Ronald Reagan.

☆

Claude Rains made his movie debut in *The Invisible Man* (1933).

☆

Charles Bronson and Humphrey Bogart both made their movie debuts at the age of thirty-one.

☆

Tom Selleck first came to the notice of the Hollywood talent scouts as the model in the billboard adverts for Salem cigarettes. As a teenager he won a four-year basketball scholarship to USC. He also had a lead speaking role with Mae West in *Myra Breckinridge* (1970), a role he would like to forget about.

☆

Actress Eve Marie Saint made her film debut in *On the Waterfront* (1954).

☆

Sylvester Stallone made his debut as a subway mugger in the 1971 Woody Allen movie *Bananas*.

☆

Producer/director Frank Capra said that when Barbara Stanwyck began her career, she gave everything she had on the first take. So he'd always shoot her scenes with multiple cameras to ensure the freshness of her performance.

☆

Lucille Ball was forty years old, with nearly seventy movies behind her, when the first TV episode of 'I Love Lucy' hit the American airwaves in 1951.

☆

Telly Savalas, born Aristoteles Savalas, was just about to take his master's degree in psychology at Columbia Univeristy when overnight he decided to drop out and work for the State Department. Eighteen months later he was working as an executive for ABC News, and won a Peabody Award. On his thirty-seventh birthday, for a lark, he thought he would audition for an acting job. To his amazement he landed the role, and a subsequent apprenticeship on live TV. He turned his hand to many different character parts in the movies. In 1962 he received an Oscar nomination for a supporting role in *The Birdman of Alcatraz*. His character Kojak grew out of a TV movie called 'The Marcus Nelson Murders.'

☆

TV star Henry Winkler made his Broadway debut in *42 Seconds From Broadway*, which closed the night it opened.

☆

In his teens James Garner modelled bathing-suits for a swimwear catalogue. It was his good looks that got him into acting. His Broadway debut was less than spectacular, as one of the silent judges in *The Caine Mutiny Court Martial* in the late 1940s. Today he is one of Hollywood's richest men in show business.

☆

America's number one funny lady Phyllis Diller made her movie debut in *Splendor in the Grass* (1960).

☆

Jodie Foster's mother (a former Hollywood press agent) took her and her brother to audition for a TV commercial in the mid 1960s. Jodie's brother missed out, but she got the job. At the age of three she became the Coppertone girl, with a dog pulling at her knickers. Later Jodie switched to TV drama roles and at ten landed the lead role in the Peter Bogdanovich TV series 'Paper Moon', which was translated from the movie starring Tatum O'Neal.

☆

Elizabeth Taylor's movie debut was not *Lassie Come Home* (1943), but *There's One Born Every Minute* (1942).

☆

Linda Evans, who played John Forsyth's wife in 'Dynasty', was given her first big acting break by him in 1957. When she was just fifteen John cast her in his smash-hit TV series 'Bachelor Father', never dreaming that some thirty years later they would play husband and wife in a world-renowned soap.

☆

In 1950 Sean Connery was a contestant in the Mr Universe Contest. During the competition he met the director of *South Pacific*, and was offered the role of Lieutenant Buzz Adams in the stage show. He accepted, and a star was born.

☆

Jane Fonda made her movie debut in *Tall Story* (1960).

☆

James Dean's first professional acting job was for a Pepsi commercial. He was paid $30, but got noticed by Hollywood.

☆

John Travolta made his movie debut in *The Devil's Rain* (1975).

☆

Here are a few well-known names along with their directors' feature film debuts: Orson Wells, at 26, *Citizen Kane* (1941); Francis ford Coppola, at 23, *Tonight for Sure* (1962); Martin Scorsese, at 26, *Who's That Knocking at my Door?* (1968); Dennis Hooper, at 23, *Easy Rider* (1969); George Lucas, at 26, *THX-113B* (1971); Oliver Stone, at 28, *Seizure* (1974); Ron Howard, at 23, *Grand Theft Auto* (1977); Nancy Walker, at 59, *Can't Stop the Music* (1980); Robert Redford, at 43, *Ordinary People* (1980).

☆

Actors' feature film debuts: Robert Blake, at 9, *Mokey* (1942); Rock Hudson, at 23, *Fighter Squadron* (1948); Robert Duvall, at 32, *To Kill a Mockingbird* (1963); David Bowie, at 21, *Virgin Soldiers* (1969); Michael J. Fox, at 19, *Midnight Madness* (1980); Timothy Hutton, at 20, *Ordinary People* (1980); Tom Cruise, at 19, *Endless Love* (1981).

☆

Actresses' feature film debuts: Julie Andrews, at 29, *Mary Poppins* (1964); Goldie Hawn, at 23, *The One and Only Genuine, Original Family Band* (1968); Diane Keaton, at 24, *Lovers and Other Strangers* (1970); Susan Sarandon, at 24, *Joe* (1970); Jodie Foster, at 9, *Napoleon and Samantha* (1972); Debra Winger, at 22, *Slumber Party 57* (1977); Daryl Hannah, at 18, *The Fury* (1978); Kathleen Turner, at 27, *Body Heat* (1981). Glenn Close, at 35, *The World According to Garp* (1982).

☆

Lauren Bacall was spotted by Howard Hawks as a model in *Harper's Bazaar*. He cast the sultry actress, aged nineteen, opposite Humphrey Bogart in *To Have or Have Not* (1944). The following year Bogie and Bacall were married.

☆

Producer John Houseman made his acting debut at the age of 71 in *The Paper Chase*.

☆

Marlon Brando made his movie debut in *The Men* (1950).

☆

Humphrey Bogart first got into acting by way of a dare. As manager of a touring play in 1920, he ticked off one of the actors about how easy an actor's life really was. Several of the actors challenged Humphrey to give it a try himself. He did, and swore he would never go on stage again!

☆

Goldie Hawn worked as a can-can dancer at the 1964 New York World Fair, then as a caged go-go dancer in New Jersey. She moved on to Las Vegas and danced in several reviews as a showgirl. It was while in Las Vegas in the late 1960s that she got her first big TV break on the series 'Laugh-In.

☆

Bette Midler's first movie was *Hawaii* (1965), in which she played a missionary's wife who suffered from sea sickness.

☆

At the tender age of twenty-three, Warren Beatty had a contract with MGM Studios, and went to Broadway to star in his first stage show. The show was a complete flop, but director Elia Kazan saw Warren in it and signed him on the spot to star in *Splendor in the Grass*, which was the start of his career.

☆

Robert De Niro made his film debut in *Hi Mom* (1970).

☆

At the age of sixty-one, Sidney Greenstreet made his movie debut in *The Maltese Falcon* (1941).

Music, Music, Music - and Musicians

At Clark Gable's thirty-sixth birthday party the studio got Judy Garland to sing 'Dear Mr Gable' to the tune of 'You Made Me Love You'. Louis B. Mayer liked the idea so much that he had it written into his 1937 movie *Broadway Melody Of 1938*.

☆

A Las Vegas promoter has booked the show room of the Las Vegas hotel for New Year's Eve, 1999. He's promoting the concert as Elvis Presley's return to showbiz, and has already sold ringside tickets.

☆

Composer Irving Berlin couldn't read music, and could play the piano only in the key of F. He composed over 3,000 songs.

☆

In the early 60s Chuck Berry spent two years in prison for income tax evasion, and was convicted of further tax evasion in the late 1970s.

☆

Within four weeks of Al Jolson's record 'Sonny Boy' hitting the American market in 1928, it had sold twelve million copies.

☆

In 1971 Vincent Damon Furnier, at the age of twenty-three, suddenly transformed himself into Alice Cooper, aptly designated by *Time* magazine as the 'King, Queen, Unicorn and Godzilla of schlock rock'.

☆

Roy Rogers the singing cowboy introduced the song 'Don't Fence Me In' in his movie *Hollywood Canteen*. Roy loved the song so much that he had it specially written into the movie at the last minute, much to the delight of Cole Porter, who wrote it only months before the movie was shot.

☆

Miss World 1963 was Miss Holland Catherina Lodders, who on 12th December 1963 married Ernest Evans, better known as Chubby Checker.

☆

Kenny Rogers was once a member of the New Christy Minstrels singing group.

☆

Singer Al Martino played the Italian Singer in *The Godfather* (1972).

☆

Singer Johnny Mathis admitted that he had eaten monkey brains during a trip to the Philippines.

☆

Carol King's 1971 Grammy-award-winning album 'Tapestry' was the largest-selling LP in history, selling 13 million copies, until Fleetwood Mac's 'Rumours' and the score for *Saturday Night Fever* came along.

☆

On 8th September 1987 Los Angeles jazz radio station KKGO agreed to pay $4,600 in back rent to save ailing clarinettist and big band leader Woody Herman, seventy-four, from being evicted from his Hollywood Hills home. Woody died a few weeks later, on October 29th.

☆

Phyllis Diller's comedy act is just that, an act – in real life she's a very accomplished classical pianist who's performed with some hundred symphony orchestras. Between 1972 and 1982, Phyllis appeared as a piano soloist, playing Bach and Beethoven at symphony concerts in Canada, Mexico, Hawaii and all over America.

☆

Charlie Chaplin wrote the songs 'Smile' and 'Limelight', two things he was very proud of all his life.

☆

Connie Francis began her show-business career playing the accordion before taking up singing.

☆

Barry Manilow had the fastest ticket sell-out in Broadway history for his concert series.

☆

On 21st January 1990 superstar Michael Jackson unveiled a painting of himself bought by a Japanese businessman for $2.1 million. At the time it was said to be the most valuable portrait of a living person. The painting depicted Michael as a modern Renaissance man, dressed in a red jacket and blue tights sitting on a stool and clasping a book, which did not have a title on its cover.

☆

Every cent earned from the song 'God Bless America' goes to the Boy and Girl Scouts of America. Irving Berlin, who wrote the song, insisted on this many years ago.

☆

Debbie Reynolds recorded a song called 'Tammy' in 1957. Nobody in the industry thought much of the song, but the public loved it and made it a smash hit.

☆

When, in the summer of 1967, John Lennon remarked that the Beatles were more popular than Jesus, it started off a string of Beatle burnings, which began in Georgia where listeners to WAYX gathered to burn Beatles records. Many radio stations around the world banned the playing of Beatles records.

☆

Jane Froman sang the songs for Susan Hayward in *With a Song in my Heart* (1952).

☆

Perry Como, the Italian/American singing star, is the seventh son of a seventh son.

☆

The mother and daughter duo 'The Judds' have been awarded the Academy of Country Music's award for Best Vocal Duo five years in a row.

☆

Before the 1935 movie *Naughty Marietta*, Forest Lawn Cemetery's theme song was 'Ah, Sweet Mystery of Life'. After the movie, they thought the song too commercial and dropped it.

☆

Ex-Beatle Paul McCartney is the proud owner of the rights to all the late Buddy Holly's songs.

☆

'White Christmas' is the largest selling song from a movie. Bing Crosby sang it in *Holiday Inn* (1942). To date it has sold 30 million copies.

☆

Art Garfunkel met Paul Simon when he played the Cheshire Cat and Paul played the White Rabbit in a grammar school production of *Alice in Wonderland*. They later found out that they grew up just three blocks away from each other in Queens. A few years later they teamed up and recorded under the name of Tom and Jerry, scraping in to the charts with a song called 'Hey – Schoolgirl'.

☆

It's rumoured that Elvis Presley once fired a gun at his TV set when singer Robert Goulet appeared on the screen.

☆

Dooley Wilson was seen in *Casablanca* (1942) playing the piano, and again as a piano player in *Higher And Higher* (1943). In reality Dooley could not play a note of music; all his playing was performed by Elliott Carpenter.

☆

In 1946 Hal Linden played the clarinet with the New York American Symphony Orchestra.

☆

In 1964 actor Lorne Greene had a number one record in America called 'Ringo'.

☆

Glen Campbell was the seventh son of a seventh son, in a family so poor that Glen had to share a bed with three of his brothers. As a young boy he sang in the Church of Christ in his home town in Arkansas, where his grandfather was the preacher. He left school at fourteen, bought a guitar and taught himself to play. From time to time he would accompany the local gospel church service. In the mid-1950s he hit the road with his own band called Uncle Boo's.

☆

Johnny Mathis's Greatest Hits album stayed on the Bill Board best-selling chart list from 1958 till 1968.

☆

At first the song 'Somewhere Over the Rainbow' was dropped from *The Wizard of Oz* (1939), because the producer thought it slowed down the pace. Months later the song was put back, and the rest is history.

☆

The song 'Nancy with the Laughing Face' was written by Jimmy Van Heusen and TV comedian Phil Silvers.

☆

Pianist Ray Charles became blind at the age of five.

☆

In New Orleans a thirteen-year-old called Louis Armstrong shot a pistol into the air, and was arrested and sent to a reform school. This changed his life; at the school, in 1913, Louis received his first training in music from a Captain Jones. A year from the day he'd been arrested, Louis formed his own band and started work around New Orleans.

☆

Barry Manilow has taken a cue from the late Joan Crawford. He has it written into his concert contract that the auditorium temperature must be in the low 60s, the same demand Joan Crawford had put into her contracts for studio filming.

☆

Diahann Carroll won a Metropolitan Opera Scholarship a few days after her tenth birthday, but when she starred in *Porgy and Bess* (1959) Loulie Jean Norman dubbed her singing.

☆

In the 1930s Errol Flynn visited Cuba, where he hired a complete orchestra to follow him everywhere. The orchestra serenaded him on all his public appearances, making the visit a real Hollywood affair.

☆

Elvis Presley's favourite movie of all time was *King Solomon's Mines* (1950), which starred Stewart Granger. Elvis had an original copy of the movie, which he would play over and over again. There was some talk of him starring in a remake in the late 1960s.

☆

Tom Jones's famous sexy gyrations incite hundreds of female fans to toss their lacy panties and room keys on stage at every show. One night at his Cesars Palace concert in Las Vegas, they collected five thousand keys from the stage. When Tom bought his beautiful brick Tudor mansion in Bel Air California, he had all his furniture shipped from his homeland, Wales. His most sentimental piece is a phone-box from his village of Pontypridd, that he once used to ring a local sweetheart from, now his long-time wife Linda.

☆

Few people know that actress Glenn Close has a great singing voice. She starred in the Broadway stage show *Barnum*, and is on the original Broadway cast album.

☆

Singer Chuck Berry has a degree in Cosmetology from an American beauty school.

☆

Bandleader Lawrence Welk has a licence plate which reads A1 AND A2, which was how he always started his music.

☆

Woody Allen was once the lead member of the New Orleans Funeral and Rag Time Orchestra, which played in New York's Greenwich Village.

☆

TV star and comic Red Skelton has composed over sixty symphonies that have all been performed by the London Philharmonic and by pianist Van Cliburn.

☆

Singer Eartha Kitt was labelled a 'sadistic nymphomaniac with a vile tongue' by the CIA for her outspoken views on politics. She once made a necklace of dead crickets for her baby daughter to cure teething pains, and always carries a clove of fresh garlic with her to ward off evil spirits.

☆

At one point in 1978 the Bee Gees tied with the Beatles' record for having five singles in the same top ten; they were all from the soundtrack for *Saturday Night Fever*.

☆

In 1989 Elton John backed top piano-makers Steinway and Sons bid to save the endangered African elephant, by not using ivory piano keys any more.

☆

Bill Howard, son of Dorothy Lamour, once managed a pop band called Dino, Desi and Billy. Desi Arnaz Jr and Dean Martin's son Dino were the other two members of the 1960 rock group.

☆

Gene Simmons, lead singer in the rock group Kiss, was born in Israel. His tongue is seven inches long.

☆

Stevie Wonder, born Steveland Morris Haraway, has been blind since birth. By the time he was ten years old he was a virtuoso on the piano, bongos, harmonica and guitar and at the age of twelve he cut his first record, 'Fingertips'.

☆

While Neil Sedaka was at high school, he was selected by Arthur Rubinstein as New York's outstanding young classical pianist. At sixteen he composed his first hit, 'Stupid Cupid', which was also a hit for Connie Francis.

☆

Herb Alpert played a drummer in Cecil B. De Mille's movie spectacular *The Ten Commandments* (1956). Ten years later, his Tijuana Brass record albums sold 13,700,000 copies.

☆

Playing the electric keyboard for the Beach Boys back in 1972 was singer Toni Tennille. She was the first and last 'Beach Girl' ever to play with the group.

☆

Singer and ukelele player Tiny Tim, who had the hit 'Tiptoe Through the Tulips' in 1968, is lefthanded and has an incredible 3½-octave vocal range.

☆

Each time the Johnny Carson 'Tonight Show' theme is played, singer Paul Anka, who wrote it, receives $200.

☆

RCA put Elvis Presley under contract in 1955 and within twelve months he had sold ten million singles. In the same year he was a guest on the Ed Sullivan TV Show. Though billed as 'Elvis the Pelvis', he was only shown from the waist up; his sexy gyrations were considered totally unsuitable for Sunday night family viewing.

☆

Rudy Vallee was the first person to record the song 'As Time Goes By'.

☆

Band leader Count Basie started out as a drummer and then switched to the piano.

☆

Actor Richard Harris had a number one record in 1968; it was 'MacArthur Park'.

☆

Neil Sedaka wrote the song 'Oh, Carol' for songwriter and childhood friend and sweetheart Carol King.

☆

Johnny Mathis once said: 'I'm scared to death of audiences. Every time I go out, the people seem to be saying, "Prove it! Prove it!" I still have the feeling of not being good enough.'

☆

CBS records honoured Michael Jackson as their label's biggest money-maker of the 1980s; his fans bought more than 110 million of his records in that decade.

☆

Jazz pianist Errol Garner is lefthanded.

☆

Elvis Presley changed to fancier lamé costumes after he saw Liberace's Las Vegas act.

☆

Rock star Billy Joel once worked as a piano player in a Los Angeles bar under the name of William Martin. His first solo album was recorded at the wrong speed, which gave him a higher sounding voice.

☆

In 1966, Herb Alpert purchased the old Charlie Chaplin Studio and opened his own company, A&M Records.

☆

Singer, songwriter and actor Mac Davis wrote the Elvis Presley hit 'In the Ghetto'.

☆

Singer Bruce Springsteen went to a strict Catholic school in Asbury Park, New Jersey, where he was asked to draw a picture of Jesus and hand it to the nun taking the class. When Bruce handed in his personally prophetic drawing of Christ crucified on a guitar, the nuns were not amused.

☆

Richard Rogers took only five minutes to write the music to 'Bali Hi' for *South Pacific*.

The Small Screen

The number one soap 'Dallas' started because David Jacobs, a New York writer of children's books, moved to Los Angeles to be near his twelve-year-old daughter, who was living with his ex-wife. He decided to write something for TV to get money in while he worked on another children's book. Two years later 'Dallas' was on the TV screen, the first evening soap series to succeed in America since 'Peyton Place' in the 60s.

The Perry Mason character was created by Erle Stanley Gardner, himself a lawyer, who died in 1970 at the age of ninety. The series first ran on CBS radio from 18th October 1943 to 1955: the original TV series ran from 1957 to 1966, then the show was picked up again in 1973 for a thirteen-week run. On 22nd May 1966 Erle Stanley Gardner appeared in the last episode called 'The Case of the Final Fade-Out'. On January 31st 1963, in an episode called 'The Case of the Constant Doyle', Bette Davis filled in playing Perry Mason while Raymond Burr was in hospital. She did not let the side down – she also won her case.

The TV series 'Cagney & Lacey' has a history arguably more amazing than the show. The series was based on the 1981 TV movie starring Loretta Swit and Tyne Daly. Because Loretta was a regular on the M*A*S*H TV series she did not want to do 'Cagney & Lacey', which is why Meg Foster played opposite Tyne in the 1982 episodes. When the show came up for another series, Meg was fired and her replacement was Sharon Gless. The series was cancelled in 1983, but the network bought it back because of its popularity. Behind closed doors at CBS the show was nicknamed 'dykes'.

☆

Every actor on the TV series 'Falcon Crest' has a setside chair with his or her name on it. When Lana Turner arrived to appear in the show, she immediately ordered her chair repainted. Instead of reading 'Lana Turner', it had to say 'Miss Lana Turner'. Until the 'Miss' was painted, Lana would not set foot on the set.

☆

In 1956 an 'I Love Lucy' Christmas TV special was made as a pilot show to sell the idea of an 'I Love Lucy' series to the CBS network. The special starred the Ricardos (Lucille Ball and Desi Arnaz) along with their friends the Mertzes (Vivian Vance and William Frawley). The network loved it, and the rest is history. But the Christmas special wasn't shown on American TV in its entirety until thirty-three years later, when CBS aired it at 8.30 pm on Monday, 18th December 1989. It rocketed into the top ratings for that week, proving again that America loved Lucy.

☆

In a 1963 interview Carol Burnett told the American *TV Guide* that she'd never do a series on TV.

☆

When the American network ABC was offered the series 'The Cosby Show' it viewed the pilot with interest but finally turned it down. The show was picked up by NBC and went on to become the most successful ever TV sitcom. It's said that ABC would have lost an estimated half a billion to a billion dollars in revenue.

☆

Until 1985 visitors to Dallas, Texas, all wanted to see the Dealy Plaza where President John F. Kennedy was assassinated. Nowadays the number one attraction is Southfork Ranch where 'Dallas' is shot on location, and the hero in Dallas these days is JR, played by Larry Hagman.

☆

TV actor Robert Stack played Eliot Ness of 'The Untouchables' in a series which stretched over seventeen years in 114 hour-long episodes. During that time he had an army of viewers worldwide, and even today, when the show has been off the air for years, fan mail for Eliot Ness still turns up at the TV studio.

☆

Bill Cosby and little Emmanuel Lewis starred in a 1983 TV commercial for Jello pudding, and the two have been friends ever since.

☆

Alan Alda, who played Hawkeye, and Loretta Swit, who played Margaret Houlihan, were the only stars to be in the series M*A*S*H from beginning to end; there were 255 episodes. M*A*S*H ran for eleven annual seasons on American TV, starting in September 1972 and ending in January 1983. It was a touch of Hollywood, since the real Korean War ran for only three years, from June 1950 till July 1953. Gary Burghoff, who played Radar, was the only member of the original movie cast to be carried over into the TV series.

The Koreans did not like the series; the director of the Korean Cultural Service in New York said in an interview with *The New York Times* that he was glad the show was ending, because 'It has been building a wrong image of Korea and its people in the minds of the American public.'

Over its years on the air the series received ninety-nine Emmy nominations and won fourteen Emmys, a selection of Golden Globes, a People's Choice Award and a number of others. The final episode was watched by 100-million-plus people in America, which beat the episode of 'Dallas' of who shot JR? American TV advertisers paid big bucks for a 30-second commercial spot in the final episode.

☆

On the soap 'The Young and the Restless' there was so much backstage hysteria about AIDS infection from kissing that in 1985 the producers brought in a medical expert to talk to the cast.

☆

American TV talk-show host Oprah Winfrey has her own TV production company called Harpo – which is Oprah spelt backwards.

☆

Philip Morris cigarettes were the sponsors of the original 'I Love Lucy' TV series in the 50s and 60s. Everybody on the series was forbidden to say the word 'lucky', because of their rival sponsor Lucky Strikes.

☆

Robert Foxworth, who plays Chase Gioberti in 'Falcon Crest', was so angered to find that Jane Wyman's studio trailer was six inches longer than his that he demanded that the studio give him one the same size, and they did, to keep the peace.

☆

Before Tom Selleck became a superstar he appeared on the American TV show 'The Dating Game' as a bachelor, and came in as second choice.

☆

The American ABC is the only TV network ever to employ a psychic to help select which shows will rate well. From 1978 till 1980 Beverlee Dean was on the payroll with a contract of $24,000 for the first year, $30,000 for the second, predicting the new winning shows. Over those two years the ABC network was number one, with shows like 'Mork & Mindy', 'Benson' and 'Taxi', which Beverlee picked to be smash-hit comedies. At the end of her contract in 1980 the studio did not renew it.

☆

When the 'Mary Tyler Moore Show' ended its long TV run, Ted Knight, who played Ted Baxter the newscaster, thought he'd try his hand at a stage show, and landed the lead in a Broadway comedy called *Some of My Best Friends*. The show closed after the opening night. Ted returned to TV in a smash-hit comedy 'The Ted Knight Show', followed a little while later by an even bigger hit, 'Too Close for Comfort'. When asked why he'd never done a Ted Baxter TV series, he said, 'I won't do a Ted Baxter spin-off. I really love the guy, but who could stand him for thirty minutes a week – I couldn't!'

☆

When they were casting for Tony Danza's role in the hit TV series 'Taxi' they were looking for an Irish heavyweight fighter, who was to be called Phil Ryan. After Tony auditioned for the role they changed his name to Tony Banta.

☆

The role of superbitch Alexis in 'Dynasty' was originally intended for Sophia Loren. Joan Collins was second choice ... but what a second choice!

☆

Lorenzo Lamas, who plays the sexy playboy Lance Cumson in 'Falcon Crest', has a weakness for fast cars. In 1977 he was in a bad crash where he cracked his skull; he was partially paralysed and couldn't speak for three days. Then in 1985 a 100-miles-per-hour racing-car smash left him with a broken collarbone and a badly dislocated shoulder.

☆

In the 1950s Louis Armstrong made a TV commercial, singing and dancing with toddlers to promote a range of dolls called 'Suzy Cute'.

☆

The Commerce Bank of Beverly Hills was made famous by the TV series 'The Beverly Hillbillies' in the 60s. The bank was run by Mr Milburn Drysdale, and it was the bank which housed the $50,000,000 of the Clampits. People started to think the bank was real, and quite a few very wealthy Beverly Hills residents inquired about depositing their fortunes with it. The power of television!

☆

As a teenager, Kate Jackson, ex-'Charlie's Angels', set her sights on becoming a professional tennis player. She got an appetite for acting after a short run in a summer stock show. Years later she came up with the idea for a TV series about three karate-chopping women detectives, the studio liked it, and 'Charlie's Angels' was born.

☆

When the network was putting together the 'Mary Tyler Moore Show' the producers sent out word that they wanted a Betty White type to play the double-edged Sue Ann Nivens, but the producers never offered the role to Betty herself. One day she sashayed in and offered herself for the role. They couldn't believe their luck.

☆

The most popular movie shown on American TV is *Casablanca*; it is also the movie which has had most reruns on TV.

☆

'I Love Lucy' TV star Vivian Vance's contract stipulated that she stay twenty pounds overweight for her role as Ethel Mertz. The show's producers and directors wanted her to look older and frumpier than Luciile Ball, even though in real life there was only thirteen days between them.

☆

Larry Hagman, who plays JR Ewing in 'Dallas', got his first taste of TV soap operas in 1961, in the afternoon show 'The Edge of the Night' in which he played a lawyer. He was with the show for three years, then left New York for Hollywood, where he played Major Tony Nelson in the smash-hit comedy series 'I Dream of Jeannie'.

☆

Robin Williams once picked up $150 dollars a day miming on the steps of the Metropolitan Museum of Art in New York at weekends. This was in the 1960s, long before he burst on to the TV screens as Mork in 'Mork & Mindy', which became the biggest TV comedy hit of 1978 and '79.

☆

The Desilu TV studio contracted Walter Winchell to narrate the series 'The Untouchables' for $25,000 per episode.

☆

Emma Samms had a dream of following in her mother's footsteps as a ballerina. But at the age of sixteen her dreams were dashed by a hip injury that threatened to cripple her for life if she didn't give up dancing. At twenty-six, she landed the role of Holly Sutton on TV soap 'General Hospital', then went on to the superstar world of Fallon in 'Dynasty'.

☆

The licence plate 'LA LAW' seen in the opening segments of the hit TV series belongs to a lawyer named Richard Niederberg, who receives a very modest fee for its use.

☆

Comedian David Brenner has guested on more TV chat shows than any other performer in America.

☆

Because of the very strict laws which protect child actors, twins are often used. In the TV series 'Bewitched', Tabitha Stevens was played by twins Erin and Diane Murphy.

☆

Carroll O'Connor played in twenty-seven movies and over 120 TV shows before he landed the role of the bigot Archie Bunker in the superhit 'All In The Family', which grossed him around three million dollars annually in the mid 1970s.

☆

In 1981, Elizabeth Taylor was the first movie superstar to have an on-going leading role in and American soap opera. The soap was 'General Hospital', where she played a widow called Helena Cassidine. She thus made soap operas respectable and many big movie stars have followed in her footsteps with guest roles.

☆

Jackie Coogan, one of Hollywood's first child stars, played Uncle Fester in TV's send-up horror series 'The Adams Family'. In the early 70s he won Emmy Awards for directing episodes of M*A*S*H and the TV series 'The White Shadow'.

☆

Mary Tyler Moore's face was never seen on the TV series 'Richard Diamond', even though she played the switchboard operator.

☆

The original Hollywood police station in Wilcox Avenue became the Metropolis police station on the old 'Superman' TV series.

☆

During the shooting of the Carol Burnett TV shows the cast and crew would run a sweepstake to see how long it would take Harvey Korman to break up in a sketch. These sweepstakes went on for years before Harvey found out, and when he did – he broke up again.

☆

Roger Moore, best remembered for his James Bond roles, once played Beau Maverick in the TV series 'Maverick'.

☆

It's rumoured that Joan Collins and Linda Evans are not exactly bosom buddies. Whenever the two stars had to make joint personal appearances for 'Dynasty', the situation got a little tense. The show's publicity director always requested that the two never be given plane seats together, and never have their hotel suites on the same floor.

☆

Before Mary Tyler Moore got the TV role of Laura Petrie in the 'Dick Van Dyke Show' in 1961, she played a three-inch-high Happy Hotpoint in a TV appliance commercial. Some twenty years later she emerged as a multimillionaire television tycoon.

☆

During a love-scene take on 'Dynasty' Michael Nader, who plays Dex, grabbed Joan Collins, who plays Alexis, and planted an exuberant kiss on her lips. The powerfully built actor didn't know his own strength in the kissing department; he badly bruised Joan's lips and she had to take the rest of the day off kissing an ice-pack.

☆

When NBC cancelled their TV series, 'The Monkees', they received more letters protesting the cancellation than for any other series they ever produced, including 'Star Trek'.

☆

In 1985 Jamie Farr, who played Corporal Clinger in M*A*S*H, fronted a TV commercial selling stick-on notepaper called Clingers. It's reported that he was paid four million dollars for doing the commercial.

☆

In 1977 Danny DeVito's on-the-spot thinking and quick wit got him the role as Louie, the smart-mouthed cab dispatcher in 'Taxi'. As soon as he entered the audition room he saw the producer's face freeze, and instantly knew he had to do something to break the ice and tension. He climbed on to the stage and growled in his deepest voice, 'Now before I start, I just gotta know one thing; who wrote this s---?' Everyone fell about and Danny was on the road to TV stardom.

☆

Lucille Ball loved to give Christmas presents to all the cast and crew on her TV series; it's said that she gave presents which were monogrammed so that if you didn't like it you could never return the gift. Bob Carroll, head writer on the series, remembers that Lucy didn't like kudos for her good work. 'She was embarrassed by any compliments,' he says. 'We used to give her a silver dollar after a particularly good episode. She liked that tradition, because it didn't involve talking about it.'

☆

William Shatner was not the first choice to play Star Trek's Captain James T. Kirk. The original choice, Geoffrey Hunter, turned the role down. He died in 1969. The role of Mr Spock was first offered to Martin Landau, who turned it down to play the lead role in a new TV series called 'Mission Impossible'.

☆

William Moulton Marston, a lawyer, invented the polygraph known as the lie detector in 1915. He also created 'Wonder Woman', which he introduced in comic book form in 1941, on which the 1970s Universal TV series was based.

☆

Joan Collins received between 11,500 – 12,000 love/hate letters per week when she was playing the bitch in 'Dynasty'.

☆

Singer/dancer Ann Miller was the first tap dancer to appear on American TV.

☆

In the 1940s the top American TV show was 'The Ed Sullivan Show'. Just about every star clamoured to be on it; some would even appear for nothing. Not so when it came to Dean Martin and his partner Jerry Lewis; they took half the talent budget of $400 as their fee when they appeared on the show in 1948, quite a fee in those days.

☆

When they were looking for a Lou Grant type for the 'Mary Tyler Moore Show' they wanted comedian Shelly Berman for the role. But Shelly wanted to continue with his comedy TV and stage performances, so the role went to Ed Asner.

☆

When the 'Cosby' series was rating number one week after week on American TV, the price of a 30-second commercial slot during the show was around $605,075. Even so there was a long waiting list of clients.

☆

At the age of fifty-two, Ronald Reagan made his last movie, *The Killers* (1964). The movie was made for TV, but was later considered too violent for the small screen, and was only shown in cinemas.

The Ones that Got Away:
ROLES THEY TURNED DOWN

Billie Burke got the role of the Good Witch Glinda in *The Wizard of Oz* (1939) after the studio's first choice, MGM starlet Helen Gilbert, chose to run off with Howard Hughes instead.

☆

James Dean turned down the lead in *The Silver Chalice* (1954), which went to Paul Newman. Then Dean beat Newman for the lead role in *East of Eden* (1955). Then came *Somebody Up There Likes Me*, and James got the lead role, but on 30th September 1955 he was killed in a car accident. His replacement was Paul Newman.

☆

The first choice to play the title role in *Scrooge* was Richard Harris, but he turned it down. The next choice was Rex Harrison, but the deal fell through at the last minute, and the part went to Albert Finney.

☆

In 1961 Laurence Olivier decided not to accept the leading role in *Judgement at Nuremburg*, so it went to Burt Lancaster.

☆

In 1940 Van Johnson was a matinee idol. In the 1950s he was offered the role of Elliot Ness in a new TV series called 'The Untouchables', but turned the role down. Next in line was Robert Stack, who starred in the show from 1959 till 1963.

☆

Anthony Newley, James Booth, Terence Stamp and Laurence Harvey all turned down the lead in *Alfie* (1966). Michael Caine was fifth choice. Cilla Black had the first hit in 1966 with the song 'Alfie' in the UK, and in 1967 Dianne Warwick's version reached the top twenty in America.

☆

First choice to play Miss Ellie in 'Dallas' was Doris Day, and first choice to play JR was Robert Kulp.

☆

At the last minute Betty Hutton stepped in and took over the starring role from an ailing Judy Garland in *Annie Get Your Gun* (1950).

☆

Albert Finney was first offered the title role in *Lawrence of Arabia* (1962). He turned the role down and it went to Peter O'Toole.

☆

Actress/dancer Cyd Charisse had to turn down *Easter Parade* (1948) because she broke her leg a matter of weeks before shooting was to start. Then in 1951 she had to give up the starring role in *An American in Paris* because she found out she was pregnant; the role went to a newcomer, Leslie Caron.

☆

Christopher Reeve turned down a million dollars to star in *American Gigolo*. When the role was offered to Richard Gere, he didn't think twice.

☆

James Mason and Bette Davis were Edward Albee's first choices to star in the movie version of the play *Who's Afraid of Virginia Woolf*, but the roles went to Richard Burton and Elizabeth Taylor, who won the Oscar for Best Actress in 1966. This was the movie which broke all the Hollywood taboos for adult material with its four-letter words.

☆

George Peppard accepted the role of Blake Carrington in 'Dynasty', but walked off the set in a huff during the filming of the pilot. The role was handed to second choice John Forsythe.

☆

Both the studio and the producers of *Lolita* (1962) desperately wanted Hayley Mills to play the lead, but at the time she was under contract to the Disney Studios and they would not release her.

☆

The original casting for *The Wizard of Oz* (1939) was: Shirley Temple as Dorothy, Buddy Epsen as the Tin Man, W.C. Fields as the Wizard. In the movie Frank Morgan got to play five roles: a guard at the door of the Emerald City, a guard at the doorway to the Wizard's Chamber, a coachman, Professor Marvel and the Wizard of Oz.

☆

In 1967 Shirley MacLaine turned down a million-dollar contract to appear in *Casino Royale*.

☆

Alan Ladd turned down the role of Jeff Rink in *Giant* (1956), thereby giving James Dean his very first movie role.

☆

Noel Coward, Michael Redgrave and George Sanders all turned down the stage role of Professor Higgins in *My Fair Lady*.

☆

Anne Bancroft was up for the role of Joan Crawford in the movie version of Christina Crawford's controversial bestseller, *Mommie Dearest*, but at the last minute she was replaced by Faye Dunaway.

☆

In 1981 Tom Selleck was into his new TV role as Magnum PI, so he turned down the lead in *Raiders of the Lost Ark*.

☆

Warren Beatty turned down flat both of the lead roles in *Butch Cassidy and the Sundance Kid* (1969).

☆

When the movie *The Jazz Singer* was offered to Eddie Cantor he turned it down, and suggested another actor called Al Jolson for the role.

☆

Susan Dey from TV's 'LA Law' and Henry Winkler, 'The Fonz', turned down the lead roles in *Grease*.

☆

Bette Davis turned down the starring role in *Come Back Little Sheba* (1952), and it went to Shirley Booth, who won an Academy Award for her movie debut as Lola. In her Oscar acceptance speech she thanked Bette for turning the role down.

☆

Trevor Howard, Richard Burton, James Mason and Peter Finch were all considered for the part of James Bond in the first Bond movie.

☆

Robert Redford has turned down the following roles: Nick in *Who's Afraid of Virginia Woolf?* (1966); Benjamin Braddock in *The Graduate* (1967); Guy Woodhouse in *Rosemary's Baby* (1968); Oliver Barrett IV in *Love Story* (1970); The Jackal in *The Day of the Jackal* (1973). He thought none of these roles was right for him!

☆

Gene Kelly's broken ankle forced him to give the lead role in *Easter Parade* (1948) over to his friend Fred Astaire.

☆

Jackie Onassis turned down a $1 million deal to portray herself in *The Greek Tycoon*. The role went to Jacqueline Bisset, who received $500,000.

☆

In the 1963 movie *Cleopatra* Laurence Olivier, Peter Finch and Trevor Howard all turned down the role of Julius Caesar, which was eventually played by Rex Harrison.

☆

Black singer/actress Grace Jones is rumoured to have turned down $50,000 an episode to star in the TV series 'The A Team'.

☆

Both Mary Martin and Elizabeth Taylor were considered for the part of Nellie Forbush in the 1958 movie *South Pacific*. Mary Martin played the role on both the West End and Broadway stages, but the movie role went to Mitzi Gaynor.

☆

Cary Grant was first choice to play in the following movies, but turned them all down: *The Third Man* (1949) – went to William Holden; *Sabrina Fair* (1954) – went to Humphrey Bogart; *A Star is Born* (1954) went to James Mason; *My Fair Lady* (1964) – went to Rex Harrison.

☆

Angie Dickinson was first offered the role of Krystle Carrington in 'Dynasty', but didn't want to act in a soap opera. Today Angie says it was one of the biggest mistakes in her career. The role went to second choice Linda Evans.

☆

In 1952 Gregory Peck turned down the lead role in *High Noon*. Gary Cooper accepted, and won the Academy Award for Best Actor. Gregory said he thought he could never do justice to the part.

☆

In the 1931 classic *Frankenstein*, the role of Elizabeth was first offered to Bette Davis. She turned it down and it went to Mae Clarke.

☆

Jennifer Jones found out she was pregnant; Greta Garbo turned it down flat; so the starring role in *The Country Girl* went to Grace Kelly. In 1954 she won the Best Actress Award for her performance.

☆

In 1946 producer Darryl F. Zanuck was looking for a strong male lead to play the king in *The King and I*. His first choices were James Mason and Robert Montgomery, but Yul Brynner got the role, his first in an American movie.

☆

Alan Alda said no to the M*A*S*H role when it was first offered to him – 'If it was going to be just hijinks on the battlefield, I wanted no part of it.' Little did he know the show would be his ticket to stardom. In 1974 Alan got the Emmy Award as the most outstanding actor in a TV series.

☆

David Niven and Bette Davis were first choices to play the leading roles in *The African Queen* (1951). Of course the roles went to Katharine Hepburn and Humphrey Bogart.

☆

Deanna Durbin was on the first list to play Dorothy in *The Wizard of Oz*, but her voice was not up to standard and she was rejected. Walt Disney personally tested Deanna for *Snow White and the Seven Dwarfs* (1937), but again she was rejected because of her voice. Walt thought it had the wrong feel to it for his Snow White.

☆

Richard Dreyfuss walked out of starring in *All That Jazz* after ten days. He was replaced by Roy Schneider.

☆

Rock Hudson was considered for the lead in *Ben Hur* (1959). Charlton Heston was slated to play Messala, but a matter of weeks before shooting started he was cast in the leading role. Messala was played by Stephen Boyd, who had to wear dark contact lenses over his blue eyes. Only Charlton was allowed to have sparkling blue eyes in the movie; the director thought it gave him more sex appeal and masculinity.

☆

The original 'Road to' movies were written for Fred MacMurray and George Burns. Bob Hope and Bing Crosby, who made the movies so popular, were second choice.

☆

In *Harlow* (1965) Ginger Rogers replaced Eleanor Parker, who replaced Rita Hayworth, who replaced Judy Garland as Jean Harlow's mother.

☆

Bing Crosby was asked to play the lead in the 'Columbo' TV series, but he turned it down and it went to Peter Falk.

☆

Audrey Hepburn said no to the leading roles in *The Diary of Anne Frank* (1959) and *The Inn of the Sixth Happiness* (1958).

☆

Steve McQueen, Warren Beatty and Marlon Brando were all very high on the consideration list for the role as the Sundance Kid in *Butch Cassidy and the Sundance Kid* (1969). But director George Roy Hill always wanted Robert Redford, and of course got his way.

☆

Matthew Broderick was first choice to play Alex Keaton in the TV series 'Family Ties', but turned it down because his father James was gravely ill in New York and Matthew did not want to leave him. The role went to an unknown called Michael J. Fox, and the rest is TV history.

☆

Kirk Douglas was among the first choices to play Blake Carrington in 'Dynasty'.

☆

As you probably know, it was because of Laurence Olivier – indirectly – that Vivien Leigh was cast in *Gone With the Wind*. William Wyler went to England to try to entice Olivier to Hollywood to make *Wuthering Heights*, not an easy task because the English star wasn't particularly interested in making American movies. Wyler said he found Olivier living with a very pretty girl whom the actor repeatedly identified as an actress.

'I knew he was hinting that I should cast her in *Wuthering Heights*,' Wyler said, 'so I offered her the part of Isabel – a supporting role. She said she didn't want to play Isabel; she wanted to play Kathy, the lead. I told her that was impossible for at least two reasons. In the first place, Merle Oberon had been cast; and in the second place, if Merle didn't play the lead, there'd be no picture. But Vivien kept insisting that she wanted to play Kathy, until I finally lost patience and said, "The role of Isabel is the best you'll ever be offered in your first American picture."'

Leigh still refused to play Isabel, but did accompany Olivier to California, where in her first American picture she played the lead in *Gone With the Wind*.

☆

The role of Nurse Ratchet in *One Flew Over the Cuckoo's Nest* (1975) was turned down by Geraldine Page, Angela Lansbury, Anne Bancroft and Colleen Dewhurst. The role went to Louise Fletcher, who won an Oscar for Best Actress.

☆

Gary Cooper was the first star considered for the leading role in the 1950s movie *Wagon Train*.

☆

George Segal walked away from the movie *10*, saying he was unhappy with the way it was being handled. The producers cast again and came up with Dudley Moore.

☆

Julie Harris was director Fred Zinnemann's first choice for the part of Alma in *From Here to Eternity* (1953), but the role went to Donna Reed who won the Best Supporting Actress Oscar.

☆

Patty Duke stepped into the role of Neely O'Hara in *Valley of the Dolls* (1967) after Petula Clark turned it down.

☆

Dark Victory (1939) was originally planned for Greta Garbo, but she saw herself more as Anna Karenina. The role went to Bette Davis as very much second choice.

☆

Because of his very thick West Indian accent, Sidney Poitier was turned down by the American Negro Theater.

☆

Henry Fonda turned down the leading role in *Network*, saying it was too hysterical for him. Just as well for Peter Finch; it was Peter's last movie, for which he was given a posthumous Oscar in 1976.

☆

The leads in *Bonnie and Clyde* (1967), *Cactus Flower* (1969), *Bob and Carol and Ted and Alice* (1969) and *True Grit* (1969) were all turned down by Tuesday Weld.

☆

Errol Flynn, Warner Baxter, Basil Rathbone, Ronald Colman and Gary Cooper were all considered for the role of Rhett Butler in *Gone With the Wind*.

☆

In 1965 Lee Marvin won the Academy Award for playing both Kid Sheleen and Tim Strawn in *Cat Ballou*. The dual roles were first offered to Kirk Douglas, who turned the idea down.

☆

President John F. Kennedy wanted Warren Beatty to portray him in *PT 109* (1963), but the studio selected Cliff Robertson for the role.

Unexpected Appearances

In *Quo Vadis* (1951) you can see a very scantily dressed Sophia Loren appearing as an extra.

☆

In *A Star is Born* (1954), a drunk staggers up and asks Judy Garland to sing 'Melancholy Baby'. The actor was just an extra, but his voice belonged to Humphrey Bogart.

☆

Koo Stark, ex-royal *amour*, can be spotted making appearances in such movies as *Star Wars* and *The Rocky Horror Show*. She was born in America, daughter of TV actress Kathi Norris and B-movie producer Wilbur Stark.

☆

Bela Lugosi left his Dracula cape behind to play the monster in *Frankenstein Meets the Wolf Man*. This was the only time Bela played Frankenstein's monster.

☆

Alfred Hitchcock always made a cameo appearance in his movies. You can see him in *Lifeboat* appearing in a weight-reducing advert.

☆

In 1939 actor/dancer Donald O'Connor played Beau Geste as a twelve-year-old in the movie of the same name.

☆

In *The Blackboard Jungle* (1955) Sidney Poitier played the delinquent high school student Gregory W. Miller; he was thirty-one at the time. Twelve years later he played the high school teacher, Mr Braithwaite, in *To Sir With Love*.

☆

In 1965 Peter Sellers produced and directed a movie which featured Lord Snowdon and Princess Margaret along with actress Britt Ekland. Peter sent it as a gift to Her Majesty Queen Elizabeth II on her thirty-ninth birthday.

☆

Before Raymond Burr became famous as Perry Mason (1957–1966) and later as Ironside (1967–1975) he was the narrator in *Godzilla* (1954).

☆

John Larroquette, star of TV's 'Night Court', was an extra in *Star Trek II: The Wrath of Khan*. Another extra on the same movie was 'Cheers' star Kirstie Alley; she wore pointed ears and John wore a crab on his head.

☆

Playing Babe Ruth in the movie *Pride of the Yankees* was Babe Ruth himself.

☆

As a young man Fidel Castro appeared in *Holiday in Mexico* (1946), talked into it by the producer and Xavier Cugat.

☆

Alfred Hitchcock's daughter appeared in *Stage Fright*, *Strangers on a Train* and *Psycho*.

☆

Helen Keller, who was deaf, dumb and blind, appeared as a pilot in *Deliverance* (1918).

☆

Davey Jones, one of the original Monkees, played the Artful Dodger in the Broadway musical *Oliver!*.

☆

Mickey Rooney played a Japanese eccentric in *Breakfast at Tiffany's* (1961).

☆

Elizabeth Taylor appeared in a close-up crowd scene in *Quo Vadis* (1951). She was also an extra, as a reveller, in *Anne of a Thousand Days* (1969), which starred Richard Burton. For neither brief appearance did she received a billing.

☆

American Olympic star Bruce Jenner had the lead role in *Can't Stop the Music* (1980).

☆

Director Steven Spielberg played a clerk in an assessor's office in his movie *Close Encounters of the Third Kind*.

☆

Jacqueline Susann, who wrote the highly successful novel *Valley of the Dolls*, appeared in a cameo role as a reporter in the 1967 movie of the same name, the only time she ever appeared in a movie.

☆

Jean Harlow played an unbilled extra in Charlie Chaplin's classic *City Lights* (1931).

☆

Walter Huston played Captain Jacoby in *The Maltese Falcon* (1942).

☆

In *The Return of Dr X* (1939), Humphrey Bogart made an appearance as a vampire.

☆

Trumpet player Herb Alpert appeared as an extra in *The Ten Commandments* (1956).

☆

Playing himself in *The Greatest Show on Earth* (1952) was circus owner John Ringling North.

☆

Here is a list of stars and the movies they appeared in without receiving any credit: Lauren Bacall – *Two Guys from Milwaukee*; Humphrey Bogart – *Two Guys from Milwaukee* and *Love Lottery*; Yul Brynner – *The Magic Christian*; Joseph Cotton – *Touch of Evil*; Richard Burton – *What's New, Pussycat?*; Vincent Price – *Beach Party*; David Niven – *Road to Hong Kong*; Boris Karloff – *Bikini Beach*.

Good Luck Charms

Some stars are very superstitious and treat their superstitions extremely seriously.

☆

Leonard Nimoy always wears an old wool hat whenever he tries out for a new part; it's the very same hat he wore when he auditioned for the role of Dr Spock in the original TV series 'Star Trek'.

☆

Bob Hope never goes on stage without a pair of old gold cufflinks which were presented to him by Paramount Studios thirty years ago. He believes they bring good luck because they carry the face of St Genesius, the patron saint of actors and comedians.

☆

Elizabeth Taylor has a passion for the colour purple, and insists that her dressing-rooms are painted violet and that any flowers sent to her dressing room must be lavender-coloured.

☆

Liza Minnelli never travels without a pair of old red slippers.

☆

Mr T always wears non-matching socks.

☆

Bo Derek always lets the phone ring four times before picking it up.

☆

Barry Manilow has a clause written into all his contracts that says: 'Nobody may cross his path from the time he leaves his dressing-room until the second he steps on stage.'

☆

Robert Morley has a good luck charm in the shape of a teddy bear, which he takes everywhere. He's had the same bear since he entered show business.

☆

Lynn Redgrave will not appear in any movie, stage show or TV series unless her teddy bear is in her dressing room.

☆

Orchestra conductor Leonard Bernstein kisses his cufflinks before every performance.

☆

For a touch of personal good luck, Sophia Loren wears something red every day.

☆

Peter O'Toole almost always wears emerald green socks; he considers this his good luck charm.

☆

William Sanderson, who plays Larry in the 'Newhart' TV show, won't make an entrance without having a quarter coin stuck in his left ear for luck.

☆

When a jet black cat crosses Zsa Zsa Gabor's path, she will walk backwards three steps, or back her car up a couple of feet if she's driving at the time.

☆

Richard Chamberlain will never allow anyone to whistle in his dressing-room. If they do, he gets them to go outside, close the door, turn round three times and then come in.

Tinseltown

Hollywood, California, was founded in 1886, when Harvey Wilcox of Kansas bought 120 acres in the Cahuenga Valley area. It was really Mrs Wilcox who gave the movie capital its name. While travelling on a train a woman told her about her summer home in Illinois, which she had named 'Hollywood'. Mrs Wilcox liked the name so much that she chose it for her husband's newly bought land. On 1st February 1887 Mr Wilcox officially filed a map for subdivision selling purposes – and a city was born.

Hollywood was a totally independent city from 1903 to 1910. In early 1910 Hollywood had 5,000 settlers, and became a district of Los Angeles. By 1930 there were over 160,000 people permanently living in Hollywood, mainly due to the quick growth of the movie industry. Hollywood boasted '350 days of sunshine' to lure film-makers to build their studios there.

☆

Beverly Hills was named by an oil explorer, Barton Green. After buying up some unnamed acreage in Los Angeles and finding no oil there, he subdivided the area for homesites, built himself a huge house, and named the area after his home town, Beverly Farm in Massachusetts.

☆

Marilyn Monroe, on Hollywood: 'It's a place where they'll pay you $50,000 for a kiss and 50 cents for your soul.'

☆

The Burbank Studios in Hollywood which house Columbia Pictures and Warner Bros. claim to have produced more motion pictures than any other single location in the world.

☆

Renowned British artist David Hockney painted the inside of the Hollywood Roosevelt's swimming pool, making it Hockney's largest painting to date and the only public pool in the world where you can swim inside a work of art. The underwater mural of blue parentheses, valued at $1,000,000, was a gift to the hotel by the artist.

☆

Author Rex Reed: 'Beverly Hills is the only place in the world where the police have an unlisted telephone number.'

☆

Orange County Airport in Los Angeles was renamed John Wayne Airport in the 70s.

☆

More stars have appeared on the stage of the Hollywood Palace Theater than on any other in Hollywood.

☆

Ava Gardner said of Hollywood: 'It's a big bore. Whoever said I like it here? All I've got from Hollywood is three lousy ex-husbands.'

☆

The oldest movie studio in Hollywood was built in 1917–18, and was known as the Peralta Studios. Today the studio is called Paramount Studios. This studio lot has had many different names over the years. In 1920 it was the Brunton Studios, then the United States Studio from 1921 to 1926, when Paramount bought it. Although most Hollywood historians claim that Rudolph Valentino made many of his movies there for Paramount, he in fact died before Paramount bought it in 1926. He made his Paramount pictures at the old Lasky Studio on Sunset and Vine Streets.

☆

Groucho Marx, when asked about Hollywood: 'Ever since they found out that Lassie was really a boy, the public has believed the worst about Hollywood.'

☆

The Lorimar Studios in Hollywood changed the name of the Robert Taylor Building after producers and tenants complained in a petition that the late actor testified before the Un-American Activities Committee against the so-called Hollywood Ten, and he was considered a supporter of the Hollywood blacklist. The building has now been renamed the George Cukor Building.

☆

Musso and Frank Grill on Hollywood Boulevard is the oldest restaurant in Hollywood. It opened in 1919 and was a favourite of writers like F. Scott Fitzerald and stars like Gloria Swanson, Mary Pickford, Douglas Fairbanks and Cecil B. De Mille.

☆

Bill 'Bojangles' Robinson taught little Shirley Temple the famous staircase dance on the stairway leading from the lobby to the mezzanine in the Hollywood Roosevelt Hotel.

☆

Judy Garland: 'Hollywood is a strange place when you're in trouble. Everyone is afraid it's contagious.'

☆

The oldest house in Hollywood is hidden by trees and heavy shrubbery in the middle of Farmers Market. It is one of Hollywood's best kept secrets. The house, built in 1852, was the birthplace of Earl Gilmore, founder of Farmers Market. Earl died in the house in 1964, in the same bed he was born in. Today his bedroom is kept exactly as it was at the time of his death.

☆

It's rumoured that Montgomery Clift stayed at the Hollywood Roosevelt Hotel while filming *From Here to Eternity*. Now, his ghost haunts the halls of the hotel playing his bugle, so the story goes.

☆

Marlon Brando: 'Hollywood is a frontier town ruled by fear and love of money. People around here are trapped by success and wealth. Hollywood is one big cash register.'

☆

Cecil B. De Mille's *King of Kings* was the first movie to be shown at Graumann's Chinese Theater, on 18th May 1927.

☆

In the 1930s Universal Studios built grandstands where tourists could watch moviemaking for just 25 cents. Because the movies were silent, the tourists used to join in, cheering their favourite hero, but this was dropped when the talkies came in.

☆

The Nestor film company was the first firm to construct a movie studio in Hollywood in 1911.

☆

The Hollywood Roosevelt has always been a very popular location for movie and TV crews. *Highway to Heaven, Simon and Simon, Hunter, Moonlighting, MacGyver, Beverly Hills Cop II, Knots Landing, Sunset* and *Sledge Hammer* are just a few of the productions which have used the hotel lobby and ballroom.

☆

Walter Winchell once said about Hollywood, 'It's a place where they shoot too many pictures and not enough actors.'

☆

The largest advertising sign in Los Angeles, perhaps even the world, is the HOLLYWOOD sign on Mount Lee, in the hills above Hollywood. Each letter stood 50 feet high. The sign was first built in 1922, at a cost of $21,000. It was erected to advertise a subdivision called Hollywoodland, but over the years the 'land' letters fell off. In 1960 the Hollywood Chamber of Commerce started to restore the sign. By public demand it was fully restored by 1973, and soon after was declared a Historic/Cultural Monument of America. During 1978 a large campaign began to save the sign. Hugh Heffner was first to help by holding a fundraising party at his Playboy mansion, which raised $45,000 to sponsor the letter Y. Soon other stars joined in. Alice Cooper sponsored one O, in memory of Groucho Marx. Gene Autry sponsored an L, Andy Williams the W. Each letter cost $27,700. Today the sign stands 45 feet high and is 450 feet long, made from baked snow-white enamel weighing some 480,000 lb. The brand new sign was unveiled to the public on 11 November 1978.

☆

In 1960 two of Hollywood High's graduates were actresses Linda Evans and Stephanie Powers.

☆

Grace Kelly, asked for her thoughts on Hollywood: 'I hated Hollywood. It's a town without pity. Only success counts. Anyone who doesn't have the key that opens the doors is treated like a leper. I know of no other place in the world where so many people suffer nervous breakdowns, where there are so many alcoholics.'

☆

Metro-Goldwyn-Mayer stands for; Metro – Marcus Loew's early film company; Goldwyn – Samuel Goldwyn; Mayer – Louis B. Mayer. The MGM lion is called Leo and the studio motto is Ars Gratia Artis – Art for Art's Sake.

☆

The world-famous Vine Street in Hollywood was so named because it once ran through Senator Cornelius Cole's vineyard.

☆

United Artists was established in 1919. The artists who 'united' were Charlie Chaplin, D.W. Griffith, Mary Pickford and Douglas Fairbanks.

☆

The first tour of Hollywood was established in 1900 by Charles M. Pierce. Today there are around 100 different tours you can take.

☆

Capitol Records Tower at 1750 Vine Street in Hollywood was the world's first circular office building when it was built in 1956 by Nat King Cole and Johnny Mercer.

☆

In its heyday there were four big movie studios in Hollywood: Columbia, Paramount, 20th Century-Fox and MGM. Today only Paramount is left in Hollywood; most of the other studios are in nearby Culver City.

☆

With the AIDS scare hitting Hollywood, many stars sought legal advice. Top Beverly Hills attorney Marvin Mitchelson had a number of actresses who wanted to know if they should refuse to do love scenes or kissing scenes with a leading man known to be bisexual or gay. One actress wanted the right to have her leading men take a blood test written into her contract, but the studio said no way. The AIDS fear rocketed through Hollywood after Rock Hudson – knowing he had AIDS – kissed Linda Evans in 'Dynasty'.

☆

The Bel Air Hotel, built in the 1920s and one of Los Angeles' most deluxe old world hotels, was the home of Grace Kelly during her Hollywood career.

☆

The movies *How Green Was My Valley*, *Planet of the Apes* and *The Sand Pebbles* were all shot in the vicinity of the Malibu Creek State Park in Los Angeles.

☆

The four Warner brothers were Harry, Jack, Sam and Albert. The Warners started on an investment of $1,000. In 1966, Jack, the last surviving brother, sold his share in Warner Bros. for $32 million.

☆

Burt Reynolds once said of Hollywood: 'In order to make it in this town and be really popular, you have to kind of go into the dumper every other year.'

☆

Many stars have performed at the Cinegrill at the Hollywood Roosevelt Hotel over the years, including Mary Martin, who played the jazz club for $35 a week. She couldn't always find a baby-sitter, so her baby son Larry Hagman would come to work with his mother.

☆

Today very few stars live in Hollywood; most live in Beverly Hills, Pacific Palisades, Malibu, Bel Air or Brentwood.

☆

The Hollywood Memorial Park Cemetery, right behind Paramount Studios, is where most of the famous names in Hollywood are buried. One of the most visited cemeteries in the world, they even give out free maps so you can find where your favourite star is buried.

☆

In 1943 Bette Davis and John Garfield founded the Hollywood Canteen to entertain World War II servicemen.

☆

Tony Curtis: 'Hollywood is the most sensational merry-go-round ever built.'

Making Their Mark:
THE WALK OF FAME, ETC.

Mann's Chinese Theater on Hollywood Boulevard was built in the 1920s at a cost of a million dollars. It seats 2,200. The first movie to be shown there was Cecil B. De Mille's *King of Kings*, on 18th May 1927. On the opening gala night they charged $2.00 per seat, a high price in those days.

☆

Immortalized in the cement at Mann's Chinese Theater are 170 hand and foot imprints of the stars. Also in the cement are: Jimmy Durante's noseprint, Betty Grable's legprint, a whisker from Monty Woolley's goatee beard, the blade imprints of Sonja Henie's ice skates, the imprint of the left side of John Barrymore's face, Al Jolson's knees, the fist of John Wayne and a champagne cork from Jack Lemmon. The first people to put their prints in the wet cement at Graumann's Chinese Theater (renamed Mann's Chinese Theater in the 70s) were Mary Pickford and Douglas Fairbanks in 1927. Some movie stars would kill to have their prints at Mann's; others, like Greta Garbo, were invited on more than one occasion but always declined.

☆

In 1942 Cecil B. De Mille was too busy working with John Wayne on *Reap the Wild Wind* to place his handprints in the cement outside Graumann's Chinese Theater. This did not put off Sid Grauman, who visited the movie set with a block of wet cement and had him place his hands in it there and then. Later he returned to his theater and placed the now dry block in the courtyard.

☆

The smallest footprint in the cement at Mann's Chinese Theater is that of Jeanette MacDonald. It measures six and a half inches from the tip of the toe to the outside of the heel. She placed it there on 4th December 1934.

☆

One of the most extensive collections of movie star autographs in the world can be seen at the Max Factor Beauty Museum in Hollywood. The Scroll of Fame has been signed by the hundreds of stars who once endorsed Max Factor products.

☆

The very first bronze star to be placed in Hollywood's famous Walk of Fame was dedicated to Joanne Woodward in 1958.

☆

Burt Reynolds became so nervous while making his footprints in the cement at Mann's Chinese Theater that he misspelled his own name.

☆

Famous stars like Howard Hughes, David O. Selznick, Lon Chaney, Steve McQueen, Jane Fonda, Clint Eastwood, Robert Redford, Dustin Hoffman, Sally Field, George C. Scott, Robert De Niro, Jack Nicholson and Meryl Streep do not have their own star on Hollywood's Walk of Fame.

☆

Stars nominated by the Hollywood Chamber of Commerce to get their star in the Walk of Fame have to pay $3,500 for the honour.

☆

The Hollywood Walk of Fame is the only footpath in Los Angeles that is cleaned six times a week.

☆

In 1989, as honorary Mayor of Malibu, forty-nine-year-old actor Martin Sheen declared the very wealthy beach community a sanctuary for the homeless of Los Angeles. In August of the same year he took his crusade to help the homeless to Hollywood's Walk of Fame. While accepting a star in his honour he said, 'The sidewalks of Hollywood are known all over the world as the Walk of Fame, but many sidewalks in America could be known as the walk of shame because of the four million homeless people residing on them full time.' Martin, flanked by his wife Janet and sons Emilio Estevez and Charlie Sheen, asked the crowd to pray with him for the 400,000 homeless children. He was the 1,897th recipient of a star on the Walk of Fame.

☆

On 6th June 1944, D-day, the Allied forces used 'Mickey Mouse' as their password. Today Mickey Mouse has his own star on the Hollywood Walk of Fame, at 6925 Hollywood Boulevard outside Mann's Chinese Theater.

☆

Roy Rogers and his famous horse Trigger both placed their prints in the cement at Mann's Chinese Theater on 21st April 1949.

☆

During World War II the most popular pin-up girl was Betty Grable, whose nickname was 'Legs'. She once had her legs insured with Lloyds of London for $250,000. Their imprints can be seen today along with her handprints and signature in the forecourt at Mann's Chinese Theater.

☆

The only alien footprints at Mann's Chinese Theater belong to the aliens from *Star Wars*: C3PO, Darth Vader and R2D2.

☆

Singer Tom Jones tossed garters to several hundred female fans during a ceremony which added his name to the Hollywood Walk of Fame. He said it was now his turn to throw the underthings, seeing his fans have thrown lingerie at him on stage for years.

Money, Money, Money - or lack of it

In *Steel Magnolias* the Olympia Dukakis character conducts interviews in a high school football locker room while young men walk around her naked. The guys who wore jockstraps received $100 a day; the ones who didn't got $150 per day.

☆

Marlon Brando received $18.5 million for just twelve days' work on *Superman* (1978) which makes him the highest paid actor in the history of Hollywood for less than two weeks' work.

☆

Elvis Presley is still very much alive at the cash register. The late King's estate now earns about $15 million a year, twice as much as Elvis made in his best year alive, according to Adweek's *Marketing Weekly* magazine in 1989.

☆

When producer Adolf Zukor turned 100 years old, Paramount Studios gave him a birthday party, at the end of which they auctioned off the candles on his cake for $1,000 each, with all the money going to charity.

☆

When Sylvester Stallone played the leading role in *The Lords of Flatbush* (1974), he says all he received in the way of payment was twenty-five free T-shirts.

☆

Faye Dunaway took a $90,000 investment bond from her fee for the Mickey Rourke movie *Barfly* to put aside for her son Liam's education. She said, 'It will be worth triple by the time he is seventeen.'

☆

Singer/actress Bette Midler once got paid in solid gold bars for a concert tour; half a million dollars' worth.

☆

Charlie Chaplin was paid $130 a week playing a Keystone cop.

☆

The cost in Hollywood of insuring a film against production delays is one to three percent of the budget. The amount paid to insurance companies for such coverages in 1988 was $300 million; the amount paid by insurance companies to irrigate the farm used in *Field of Dreams* during the 1988 drought was $200,000, and to replace Sean Young with Kim Basinger in the first *Batman* movie was $500,000.

☆

Tarzan of the Apes, was the first Hollywood movie to gross over one million dollars. It starred the first Tarzan, Elmo Lincoln.

☆

The double bed used by Marilyn Monroe and Joe DiMaggio during their brief marriage fetched $25,000 at an auction in New Jersey in 1989.

☆

When Dustin Hoffman arrived in New York in the 50s to study at the Lee Strasberg Actors Studio, he was so broke he slept on Gene Hackman's kitchen floor. He took work waiting on tables, and on his days off he typed up entries for the New York yellow pages to get money for his acting classes.

☆

When the American TV series 'Happy Days' went on air in the 70s, its star Henry Winkler, who played The Fonz, was paid about $750 per episode. The series was an overnight success, and the next season he signed a contract which gave him an estimated $80,000 per episode plus a cut of the profits.

☆

In 1925 Hollywood made its most expensive silent movie, Fred Niblo's *Ben Hur*, which ended up costing $3.9 million, a fortune in those days.

☆

In the 1930s Mae West brought Paramount Studios out of the red and into the black with her movies. Some say she saved the studios.

☆

When Sylvester Stallone sold the screenplay for *Rocky*, he was working as a lion's cage cleaner with only $160 in his bank account.

☆

Hollywood costume designer Edith Head designed the most expensive movie costume, in mink and sequins, for Ginger Rogers in *Lady in the Dark* (1944). The gown cost Paramount Studios $35,000. Nineteen years later, Elizabeth Taylor's gown in *Cleopatra*, made from 24-carat gold cloth, cost $65,000 and her wardrobe budget for the movie was the highest ever spent for a single performer in any one movie – $194,000.

☆

There is a shop in Melrose Avenue, LA, called A Star Is Worn, which sells used clothing of the stars. Every garment has a tag with the owner's name on it along with the price; for example, Marlon Brando's breeches for *Mutiny On The Bounty*, *$1,000*, and John Travolta's autographed suit for *Saturday Night Fever* and the cover shot on *Time* magazine, $2,500. Sometimes the store accepts clothing from the stars on consignment. Most of them give their share of the sale to charity.

☆

As a struggling actress, to make extra money Lindsay Wagner used to babysit Glen Campbell's children. Later she struck gold with the TV series 'The Bionic Woman'.

☆

In 1985 Bill Cosby and Joan Rivers battled in a New York auction house for a set of Tiffany silverware, bidding against each other for quite a few minutes. Bill came out on top with $95,000.

☆

After the San Francisco earthquake in 1989 Paul Newman donated $250,000 to the victims. He also ordered his company, Newman's Own, to provide about 10,000 pounds of spaghetti to the thousands of homeless in Watsonville, California, which was very near the epicentre of the quake. Since Paul started his company in 1982, it's donated more than $22 million to various charities.

☆

Here are some prices paid for stars' worn-out autographed sneakers at a 1989 special Olympics benefit auction in Hollywood.

Sean Penn's $50	James Belushi's $50
Jane Fonda's $100	Demi Moore's $100
Shelly Long's $150	Burt Reynolds's $200
Brooke Shields's $200	Michael J. Fox's $250
Robert De Niro's $450	Elizabeth Taylor's $500
Johnny Carson's $550	Mick Jagger's $2,200

The top price was for Madonna's, which, believe it or not, went for $4,500.

☆

In 1934 Robert Taylor signed a contract with MGM for $35 a week, which made him the lowest paid contract player of all time. He stayed with the studios for twenty-five years, longer than any other major Hollywood filmstar.

☆

In August 1970 Zsa Zsa Gabor was attacked in a lift of New York's fashionable Waldorf Towers and robbed of jewels worth $450,000.

☆

Bing Crosby, Frank Sinatra, Joe DiMaggio, Bob Hope, Arthur Godfrey and Red Skelton all sold newspapers when they were schoolboys, to earn pocket money.

☆

Robert Redford bought the movie rights to *All the President's Men* for $450,000. He also starred in and produced the movie.

☆

The 'Cosby Show' holds the record for the highest earning TV syndication rights for a sitcom. In 1986 the rights were sold for a fee that will eventually be between half and a billion dollars.

☆

In the history of TV around the world, no one has produced more hours of prime-time TV or made more money from his shows than Aaron Spelling. In 1968 he launched his first big series, 'The Mod Squad'. His current wealth is judged to be around 335 million dollars. Every time 'Hotel', 'The Love Boat', 'Fantasy Island', 'Charlie's Angels' or 'Dynasty' is shown his income ticks upwards. Not bad for a man who came to Hollywood and got a job doing airline ticketing at the airport.

☆

In August 1989 Australian restauranteur Janette Wilkins bought a dress worn by Marilyn Monroe for $12,000 in an auction at Christie's in London. The dress was worn by Marilyn while touring United States bases in Korea. The two-piece, skin-tight, silk-crepe cocktail dress went on show at her Melbourne restaurant.

☆

In 1944 Cary Grant gave his entire salary of $100,000 from *Arsenic and Old Lace* to US War Relief.

☆

In 1989 a selection of Marilyn Monroe's personal items was placed under the auction block. This is what they fetched: A sterling silver jewellery box given to her by Jack Benny, and engraved 'Thanks Marilyn. Jack Benny' – $5,000; a plain cigarette case gifted to Marilyn by Clark Gable while they were filming *The Misfits*, engraved 'To Marilyn, Love Clark, Rino 1960' – $10,000; a brass charm bracelet from her Aunt Lowry, with two small hearts hanging from it, engraved 'To Marilyn, Love Aunty Lowry' – $3,500; a small mother-of-pearl hair comb given to Marilyn by the producer of *Bus Stop*, engraved 'Marilyn, use at any bus stop, John Logan' – $5,000; a sundial from her Brentwood home (the one she died in), which Marilyn bought on a visit to Japan in 1954 – bought by a major Japanese company for $20,000; a large embroidered black and white scarf with Marilyn's name worked into the design – $2,500.

☆

Vivien Leigh won an Oscar in 1939 for Best Actress in *Gone With the Wind*, but her acting fee was a paltry $15,000.

☆

MGM once held a huge garage-type sale which lasted three weeks. The studio sold off tons of movie props, costumes, and so on, and made four million dollars simply by selling cast-offs.

☆

Jack Klugman was the youngest of six children born to poor Russian immigrants in south Philadelphia. When he arrived in New York looking for acting work he stayed in a $14-a-month apartment with fellow struggling actor Charles Bronson.

☆

$3.5 million was the highest price ever paid by Hollywood for the rights to make a movie. It was paid to William P. Blatty for *The Exorcist*.

☆

The shirt Rudolf Valentino wore in *Son of the Sheik* (1926) was sold for $600 to a magician who now wears the shirt in his act.

☆

Cleopatra (1963) starring Elizabeth Taylor and Richard Burton cost $12 million to make.

☆

The two lowest paid stars in *The Wizard of Oz* were Judy Garland and the dog Toto.

☆

As a child star Shirley Temple reportedly earned more than $20 million for 20th Century-Fox, to whom she was under contract.

☆

At a 1989 Hollywood auction fans bought the following items of memorabilia: George Reeves' Superman costume from the 1950s TV series for $12,000; Clark Gable's white suit worn in *Gone With the Wind* for $24,000; a signed postcard from Marilyn Monroe for $18,000.

☆

It's thought that Yoko Ono – Mrs John Lennon – is the wealthiest woman in American show business, with assets of $200 million plus. In second place is singer/actress Pia Zadora, who is worth $200 million – without the plus!

☆

Pierino Roland Como was born 18th May 1912, the seventh son of a seventh son, and endured a poverty-stricken childhood. His father worked the clock round in the local mill to support thirteen children; at the age of fourteen Pierino worked in his own barbershop, where he would sing to his customers. Later he changed his name to Perry Como and took up singing full time.

☆

The fee paid for the use of a private home in Bedford, New York, for the filming of *Fatal Attraction* was $500 per day.

☆

Ben Hur (1959) won eleven Oscars, and earned $36.6 million at the box office. It was also judged one of the best films of '59 by the *New York Times*.

☆

In December 1989 Christie's in New York auctioned the dress that Judy Garland wore for publicity shots in *The Wizard of Oz*. It went to a collector for $19,800, $4,000 more than the previous record for a Judy Garland movie costume. The gallery's pre-sale estimate of the dress's value was $10,000 to $15,000. At the same auction a collector paid $275,000 for a pair of Italian eighteenth-century rococo walnut commodes used in the 1950s MGM movies *Susan Slept Here* and *Slightly Scarlet*.

☆

Ex-Beatle Paul McCartney is estimated to make about $50 million a year.

☆

When Olivia de Havilland starred in *The Well Groomed Bride* (1946), which was shot at Paramount Studios, she earned not a cent. At the time she was under contract to Warner Bros. and could not be paid by another studio. Her agent talked her into taking the role for no fee, as she thought it would keep her in the public eye.

☆

Goldfinger, the third James Bond movie, made $10 million in its first fourteen weeks. At the time it was the fastest moneymaker in the history of the movies.

☆

Mary Pickford was the first woman in America to earn one million dollars; Gloria Swanson was the second.

☆

The famous nude picture of Marilyn Monroe in her days as an unknown in Hollywood was taken by a photographer called Tom Kelly, who was paid $500 for the print by a calendar company; Marilyn was paid $50, the calendar company netted $750,000. Today the original print and neg would be worth quite a few dollars.

☆

The witch's hat worn by Margaret Hamilton in *The Wizard of Oz* (1939) sold at a Hollywood auction for $33,000. A pair of Dorothy's ruby slippers worn by Judy Garland were sold to a collector for $165,000. Clark Gable's personal script from *Gone With the Wind* sold for $77,000.

☆

Elvis Presley always kept $1 million in his personal cheque account.

☆

Warner Bros. paid $52,000 for Sean Connery's hairpiece in *Never Say Die*. To date this is the most expensive toupee ever made for a Hollywood star, and paid for by a studio.

☆

The world record for the most money lost on the making of a movie goes to *Heaven's Gate* directed by Michael Cimino, which lost $34.5 million.

☆

In 1945 Claude Rains was paid one million dollars for his role in the movie *Caesar and Cleopatra*. He was the first British actor ever to receive a million-dollar fee.

☆

In February 1990 model Jerry Hall turned auctioneer in London and put Marilyn Monroe's skimpiest swimsuit under the hammer. The jet black, hand-sequinned suit, along with its white bathing cap, sold for $9,812. The buyer was a record company promoting the career of twenty-two-year-old Marilyn lookalike, Pauline Bailey. Jerry Hall was selected as auctioneer because she had just opened in London's West End production of *Bus Stop*, in the role Marilyn made famous in the 1956 Hollywood movie of the same name.

☆

When Dustin Hoffman starred as Benjamin Braddock in the smash hit *The Graduate* (1967), he received $17,000 for his role. After the movie Dustin couldn't find acting work and collected unemployment insurance. The movie went on to gross over $50 million.

☆

The most sought-after item of Elvis Presley memorabilia from the 1980s is a 45 rpm record given away to people who toured his home in Tupelo, Missouri, in August 1982. Only 7,500 copies were handed out, and the record was never released commercially. They're now worth around $300 each.

☆

When James Cagney played Eddie Foy in *The Seven Little Foys* (1955) he refused a fee of any kind out of respect for the memory of Eddie Foy, who had befriended him in his youth.

☆

In 1937 Louis B. Mayer, head of MGM, was the highest paid person in the United States. He earned $1,296,000 in that one year.

☆

The closing credits in the 1979 *Star Trek* movie cost more to make than the movies *Friday 13th* and *Airplane* combined.

☆

MGM once insured the dancing legs of Fred Astaire for one million dollars each.

☆

Remember all those diamonds Mae West wore in her movies? Well it looks as though they could have been all fakes! Mae told everyone they were real and worth millions, but in 1989 it was revealed that she had sold the real diamonds to raise money for the war effort back in the 1940s. Mae wanted no praise, and asked that her donation be kept a secret.

☆

Early posters for the *Star Wars* sequel used the original title, *Revenge of the Jedi*. By the time it was retitled *Return of the Jedi*, some posters had already been printed, and they're now worth around $400 to avid collectors.

☆

In 1989 the pinafore Judy Garland wore in *The Wizard of Oz* was auctioned at Christies for $20,000.

☆

Jaws was the first movie to top $100 million in ticket sales.

☆

Hollywood's first child star Jackie Coogan (who played the title role in Charlie Chaplin's *The Kid* in 1921) was a millionaire by the age of six and was broke by twenty-three, after his mother squandered his fortune. This inspired the first laws to protect child actors and their earnings.

☆

In 1935 Mae West was listed as the highest paid woman in America; her estimated earnings were around $500,000.

☆

If Errol Flynn could have raised more financial backing to complete his 1953 movie *William Tell*, he would have made Hollywood history with the first movie filmed in Cinemascope. He abandoned the movie after shooting only thirty minutes of it, because he ran out of money.

☆

Jack Nicholson is rumoured to have been paid a cool $11 million for his role as the Joker in *Batman* (1989).

☆

In 1988 a script copy of *Gone With the Wind*, autographed by thirty-two persons connected with the movie, fetched $22,000 at auction.

☆

In 1980 Larry Hagman became the highest-paid star on any prime-time soap. The Lorimar production company gave in to Larry's financial demands and agreed to pay him a whopping $75,000 per episode.

☆

CBS paid $15 million for the TV rights to the movie *Star Wars*, which is still the highest price ever paid for a movie by a television network.

☆

A set of the late Judy Garland's false eyelashes sold at auction for $125, in 1979.

☆

Elizabeth Taylor was the first movie star to demand one million dollars, for her role in *Cleopatra* (1963).

Stars in Print

When Burt Reynolds posed nude as *Cosmopolitan* magazine's first celebrity centrefold in 1972 a Chicago woman bought 500 copies of the magazine, which cost her $700, to wallpaper her bedroom. Burt said, 'For $700 I would have gone over and seen her myself!'

☆

Jean Harlow wrote a novel in 1934 called *Today is Tonight*. It was not published until 1965.

☆

'Mae West' was the name given by the British RAF to their inflatable life-jackets during World War II. Even today it's recognized by compilers of dictionaries. This makes Mae West the only movie star ever to be listed in a dictionary, something she was always very proud of.

☆

Jean Stapleton, who played Edith Bunker in the TV series 'All in the Family', was voted *People* magazine's top female star of 1979 by their readers.

☆

English born actor Ray Milland's autobiography, published in 1974, was entitled *Wide-Eyed in Babylon*.

☆

Fred MacMurray's face was used as the model for the comic book hero Captain Marvel.

☆

Susan Hayward, Ginger Rogers, Gloria Swanson and Lauren Bacall have all posed as photographic models for Sears Roebuck's annual catalogue.

☆

On 4th March 1974, Mia Farrow was on the very first cover of *People* magazine.

☆

The Moon's a Balloon, the first volume of David Niven's autobiography, was dedicated to someone named Kira Kanuphyladafodilos.

☆

In 1954, a novel by Ian Fleming called *Casino Royale*, about a British agent known as James Bond, sold only 7,000 copies in its first printing.

☆

Peter Sellers was the first male to appear on the cover of *Playboy* magazine in America.

☆

During her last years at the Thomas Jefferson High School, Shelley Winters was editor of the school newspaper.

☆

In 1914 Edgar Rice Burroughs introduced his character Tarzan of the Apes, who ultimately starred in twenty-five books, movies and comic strips and was translated into fifty-six languages around the world.

☆

Lucille Ball holds the record for appearing on the cover of America's *TV Guide*; twenty-four times in all, including the very first issue in 1952, on which she was pictured with her newborn son, Desi Arnaz IV.

☆

Every Frenchman Has One is the title of the 1960 autobiography by Olivia de Havilland.

☆

Grace Kelly was the first movie star to appear on a postage stamp.

☆

William Hopper, son of Hollywood gossip columnist Hedda Hopper, played Paul Drake in the TV series 'Perry Mason'.

☆

Fred Astaire's autobiography, published in 1960, was entitled *Steps in Time*.

☆

The first American actress to appear on the cover of *Life* magazine was Jean Harlow on 3rd May 1937.

☆

Eva Gabor was the first Gabor sister to come to America in the 1930s, and she quickly launched herself as a minor star. She speaks English, French, German and Hungarian, plays the piano extremely well, and entitled her biography *Orchids And Salamis* (1951). When asked to explain the title, she said, 'Simple, dahling, because all I ever seemed to have in my fridge were orchids and salamis.'

In her major TV role as Lisa Douglas, the socialite wife who finds herself down on the farm in 'Green Acres' (1965–1971), she wore all her own gowns.

☆

In 1978, at the age of sixty, singer/actress Lena Horne was ranked alongside Elizabeth Taylor and Farrah Fawcett as one of the ten most beautiful women in the world by the magazine *Harper's Bazaar*.

☆

Hedy Lamarr published her autobiography in 1967, entitled *Ecstasy and Me*.

☆

At the age of nineteen, novelist Barbara Cartland was the gossip columnist on the *Daily Express* newspaper in England. She wrote her first book at twenty-one and to date has written around 400. She dictates 7,000 words per day, and has a daily intake of honey along with seventy vitamin pills.

☆

Marilyn Monroe appeared on the first cover of *Playboy* magazine.

☆

In 1959 singer/actor John Davidson worked as a model for Sears Department Store. He can be seen in their 1959 catalogue modelling men's underwear.

☆

In 1953 Bing Crosby wrote his autobiography and called it *Call Me Lucky*.

☆

Richard Chamberlain, who played Dr Kildare on TV, was erroneously listed twice in the fortieth edition of *Who's Who in America*.

☆

Publisher Hugh Heffner first wanted to call his new magazine *Stag Party*, but a magazine called *Stag* objected, so Hugh settled for his second choice, *Playboy*. Hugh once worked in the subscription department of *Esquire* magazine, but walked out to start up his own magazine when they refused to raise his salary from $60 to $85 per week.

☆

John Lennon was on the first cover of *Rolling Stone* magazine in November 1967.

☆

Jerry Comeaux, the stuntman in *Live and Let Die* (1973) went into the *Guinness Book of Records* when he jumped his racing boat 110 feet over a road.

☆

Tony Curtis has been billed as James Curtis, Anthony Curtis, and Tony Curtis in different movies. In 1977 he wrote a bestselling novel called *Kid Andrew Cody and Julie Sparrow*.

☆

Charlie Chaplin was on the first cover of *Time* magazine, on 6th July 1925.

☆

In December 1989 Sean Connery was voted 'the sexiest man alive' by *People* magazine. The vote for sexiest second-generation actor went to Jeff Bridges.

☆

Actress Drew Barrymore was paid a $250,000 advance to write her life story. At fourteen she holds the record for the youngest autobiographer of all time.

☆

Fabian, the 1960s pop singer, posed nude for the centrefold of an early 1970s *Playgirl* magazine.

☆

When *Blood Feast* (1963) was previewed, the movie publicist issued every member of the press with a paper bag to be sick into.

☆

In 1976 bandleader Cab Calloway wrote the biography of Minnie the Moocher.

☆

Steve Bond, who plays Jimmy Lee Holt in TV's 'General Hospital,' once posed nude for *Playgirl* magazine, eight years before he became a TV star. As soon as Steve appeared in the top rated soap, *Playgirl* republished the pictures, cashing in on his new found popularity.

☆

In 1983 ET the extra-terrestrial was runner-up for *Time* magazine's Man of the Year award.

☆

In mid-1967, Jacqueline Susann's novel *Valley of the Dolls* set a record by selling 6,800,000 copies of the paperback edition in just six months.

☆

During 1965 and 1966 actress Raquel Welch was nick-named the Cover Girl. In that time she appeared on the covers of 108 magazines.

☆

Even though writer Dorothy Parker was on her honeymoon, her editor, Harold Ross of *The New Yorker*, was pressing her for copy. She sent him a telegram which read: 'Too fucking busy, and vice versa.'

☆

Marilyn Monroe has had more books and articles written about her than any other actress or actor. Most were written after her death in 1962.

☆

William Randolph Hearst gave very strict orders to his staff that every Hearst newspaper was to mention at least once a day the name of his mistress and protegée, actress Marion Davies. For thirty years every one of his newspapers carried her name every day, even when she retired from the movie screen. In 1951 William died, and the retired actress was never mentioned in a Hearst newspaper again, until her death notice in 1961.

☆

Elizabeth Taylor became the favourite cover girl of *Life* magazine. Over twenty-five years she appeared on their cover eleven times, still a record for a film star.

☆

Errol Flynn wrote two autobiographical books, the first called *Beam Ends* and the second *My Wicked, Wicked Ways*.

☆

Actress Stella Stevens appeared as the playmate centrefold in the January 1960 issue of *Playboy* magazine.

☆

The original name for the comic strip 'Dick Tracy' was to have been 'Plain Clothes Tracy.'

☆

In July 1978 John Travolta became the first male to have his picture on the cover of *McCall's* magazine in one hundred years.

☆

Linda Goodman, world-famous astrologer and author, wrote her best-selling books *Sun Signs* and *Love Signs* in suite 1217 at the Hollywood Roosevelt Hotel. Her newest book *Star Signs* was recently completed in the same suite for good luck.

☆

British actor Christopher Lee entitled his autobiography *Tall, Dark and Gruesome*.

☆

Leon Uris, author of the book *Exodus*, failed English three times at high school.

☆

When Shelley Winters wrote her autobiography she named Errol Flynn, Marlon Brando and William Holden as some of her lovers.

☆

Joan Collins was voted Miss Press Clippings in 1982 and wore a dress to the press conference made from all the newspaper stories which had been written about her that year.

What They Did Before, and After

Cary Grant's very first job in America was as a $5-a-day stiltwalker at the Coney Island fairground.

☆

In the early 1940s Charlton Heston was a nude model for the Art Student League in New York. He earned a mere $1.25 per hour.

☆

Sean Connery, the Scottish-born actor who put James Bond firmly on the movie screen, was a male model, a coffin polisher, a bricklayer and a milkman before he got into acting.

☆

Robert Redford once served as sewer commissioner for the Provo Canyon in Utah.

☆

In 1926 Ronald Reagan served as a lifeguard. In that year he claims to have saved seventy-seven people from drowning.

☆

Before Steve Martin got his big break in show business, he spent eight years selling Davy Crocket coonskin hats and Mouseketeer ears at Disneyland. He started earning $1,500 a week as a scriptwriter for TV personalities like Sonny and Cher, Glen Campbell, John Denver, Dick Van Dyke and the Smothers Brothers before he got into acting.

☆

Carol Burnett was once an usherette at Graumans Theater in Hollywood, until she got the sack.

☆

Before Gregory Peck became an actor he worked as a carnival barker at the 1939 World's Fair, then as a tour guide at New York's Rockefeller Center, giving him extra money for acting classes.

☆

Clayton Moore, who played the Lone Ranger on television for several seasons, was noticed and signed up by a Hollywood talent scout while working as a circus trapeze artist.

☆

To supplement his early days in show business, pianist Victor Borge played the organ at funerals.

☆

Glen Ford's first real job was as manager of a burlesque house in San Francisco. It was through this job started his interest in show business.

☆

When Veronica Lake's movie career dried up she turned to bar work in California; Eleanor Powell became a Sunday school teacher; George Raft took up a job as a VIP greeter at the Riviera Hotel in Las Vegas; Jane Russell founded an agency to help couples adopt foreign children.

☆

Andy Griffith was a schoolteacher before becoming an actor.

☆

Movie producer Sid Luft, one-time husband of Judy Garland, was once a test pilot for the Douglas Aircraft Company of America.

☆

Before becoming a professional musician and bandleader, Eddie Duchin was a pharmacist.

☆

Steve Reeves, once the most muscular movie star Hollywood had ever seen, was the holder of the title Mr America in 1947. And quite a few Miss Americas have gone on to Hollywood stardom: Rosemary LaPlanche (1941); Jean Bartel (1943); Lee Meriwether (1955); Phyllis George (1971); Lynda Carter (1974).

☆

Cowboy actor Gene Autry, now a millionaire, once worked as a telegraph operator in his youth.

☆

Many other actresses have to thank the beauty queen business for their start in the movies. The following titles brought these girls to the notice of the Hollywood studios.

Lauren Bacall:	Miss Greenwich Village 1942
Joan Blondell:	Miss Dallas 1929
Anita Bryant:	Miss Oklahoma 1959
Dyan Cannon:	Miss West Seattle 1957
Claudia Cardinale:	The Most Beautiful Italian Girl in Tunis 1956
Jeanne Crain:	Miss Long Beach 1941
Yvonne de Carlo:	Miss Venice Beach 1941
Donna Douglas:	Miss New Orleans 1957
Anita Ekberg:	Miss Sweden 1951
Zsa Zsa Gabor:	Miss Hungary 1936 (but disqualified when they found out she was under sixteen years of age)
Shirley Jones:	Miss Pittsburgh 1951
Sylvia Kristel:	Miss TV Europe 1973
Dorothy Lamour:	Miss New Orleans 1931
Gina Lollobrigida:	Miss Italy 1946
Sophia Loren:	Princess of the Sea 1948 and Miss Elegance 1950
Jayne Mansfield:	Miss Photoflash 1952
Vera Miles:	Miss Kansas 1948
Kim Novak:	Miss Deepfreeze 1953
Debbie Reynolds:	Miss Burbank 1948
Cybill Shepherd:	Miss Teenage Memphis 1966
Elke Sommer:	Miss Viareggio 1959
Raquel Welch:	Miss Photographic 1953, when she was just thirteen.

☆

James Stewart began playing the accordion at a very early age. This was to be his career, until he began taking an interest in acting.

☆

As a starving young actor in New York Ken Kercheval, who plays Cliff Barnes in 'Dallas', supported himself by taking pictures of his actor friends for their portfolios. Two of his earliest customers were Robert Duvall and Dustin Hoffman.

☆

Rossano Brazzi, who starred in *South Pacific*, studied law at the University of San Marco before becoming an actor.

☆

Marlon Brando said in an interview that his earliest career goal was to be a minister.

☆

Buster Crabbe, who played the original Flash Gordon, moved into stockbroking when his career came to an end. Later he opened his own swimming pool company in California.

☆

James Cagney's first job was as a dancer in a female impersonator's act.

☆

Anthony Quinn formed his own theatre company at the age of fifteen. Before that he worked as a dress cutter and fruit picker in Los Angeles.

☆

Michael Gross, who played the dad in TV's 'Family Ties', worked as a railroad engineer, serviced machinery that made tin cans, worked in a shampoo factory, as a part-time waiter, a bank teller and a part-time shop assistant before he hit the big time.

☆

Comedian Bob Newhart was an accountant before his first comedy record (which he made as a bet) launched him into full-time show business.

☆

After getting out of the Marines, Lee Marvin cleaned chicken houses and septic tanks for a living.

☆

Jaclyn Smith started ballet at the age of three. Her love for ballet inspired her to set up a ballet school for underprivileged children in New York's Upper West Side slums.

☆

Greta Garbo's very first paying job was that of a soap latherer in a barber shop, when she was thirteen.

☆

Kiss singer Gene Simmons once taught English at a Spanish Harlem grammar school in New York City.

☆

King of the horror movies, Vincent Price, was once the art purchaser for the Sears Roebuck company in Los Angeles. Art has been a great passion of his for many years.

☆

Before he hit the big time in Hollywood, Alan Alda worked as a clown, a cabdriver and a doorman and at one point even coloured baby photographs for a living.

☆

Author Raymond Chandler was an oil company executive before he wrote *The Big Sleep*.

☆

The best known and most successful ex-Hollywood actor is Ronald Reagan, who went from B-grade movies to twice becoming the governor of California, and one of the longest reigning Presidents of the United States.

☆

Actor Ben Kingsley's first job after leaving school was as a penicillin tester for ICI. He quit the job in the early 60s to start acting. He then went to a theatre school and earned $20 per week.

☆

Long before he thought of becoming an actor, Bob Hope had a very short career as a prizefighter. His next move was into vaudeville.

☆

Actor Allen Jones is a fully-trained dentist.

☆

TV actor Jack Lord of 'Hawaii Five-O' fame is an accomplished artist; his work has been displayed at the Metropolitan Museum of Art in New York.

☆

We all think of Vivien Leigh as Scarlett O'Hara in *Gone With the Wind*, but long before her famous role she was a model for *Vogue* magazine. She was born in Darjeeling, India.

☆

During his acting dates George Hamilton ran a flower shop in the heart of Palm Beach, catering to the social set.

☆

Bob Crane, who played the lead in TV's 'Hogan's Heroes', was once a drummer with the Connecticut Symphony Orchestra.

☆

Singer/actress Debbie Harry from the pop group Blondie once worked as a Playboy bunny.

☆

Long before Patty Duke became a TV star, she appeared in a series of TV commercials for an American food company, promoting Ronzoni spaghetti.

☆

Stan Laurel was an understudy to Charlie Chaplin for many years before he teamed up with Oliver Hardy.

☆

At seventy-five Gloria Swanson started a brand new career as a sculptress. In the years to follow she had her works on exhibition at some of the world's leading galleries, including the Hamilton Gallery in London in 1979.

☆

Danny Kaye was the holder of a commercial pilot's licence, and if called on could have piloted a 747 Jumbo jet.

☆

During the last twenty years of his life, Cary Grant became a corporate executive with the Fabergé cosmetic company, and travelled the world as their ambassador.

☆

Brigitte Bardot won an excellency award from the Paris Conservatoire in ballet. Later she performed ballet on several French TV shows.

☆

Both Burt Lancaster and Yul Brynner joined the circus in their teens, and worked as acrobats. Burt formed an act with Nick Cravat, a character actor who later appeared with him in several movies. Burt was a great help to his fellow stars when he landed the role in *Trapeze*.

☆

Sylvester Stallone was once a trainee beautician, but got thrown out of a New York beauty school when he was nineteen. Later he became a gym instructor at a Swiss boarding school for girls, then studied acting at the University of Miami. His first Broadway show was *Score*, a nudie musical review.

☆

Here's how some other stars made their livelihoods before they became famous.

Dana Andrews:	an accountant with the Gulf Oil company
Lauren Bacall:	usherette in a Manhattan theatre
Warren Beatty:	rat catcher
William Bendix:	ran a grocery store
Humphrey Bogart:	US marine
Ernest Borgnine:	in the US Navy
Clara Bow:	doctor's receptionist
Chares Bronson:	coal miner earning a dollar a ton in Pennsylvania
James Caan:	rodeo rider
Michael Caine:	meat porter at Smithfield Market
Maurice Chevalier:	worked for an electrician
Chuck Connors:	professional baseball player for the Los Angeles Angels
Joan Crawford:	laundry girl
Nelson Eddy:	helped out on a switchboard
Douglas Fairbanks:	worked for an American soap manufacturer
Errol Flynn:	policeman in New Guinea
Glen Ford:	bus driver
Clark Gable:	telephone repairman
James Garner:	gas station attendant
Greer Garson:	worked for an advertising agency
Janet Gaynor:	movie usherette
John Gilbert:	door-to-door salesman of rubber goods
Sydney Greenstreet:	tea planter in India
Alec Guinness:	wrote advertising copy for an ad agency

Oliver Hardy:	movie theatre manager
Rock Hudson:	postman
Lauren Hutton:	Playboy bunny and cosmetic model
Glenda Jackson:	shop assistant at Boots in London
Alan Ladd:	ran his own hot dog stand
Dorothy Lamour:	lift operator for the department store Marshall Field in Chicago
Burt Lancaster:	lingerie salesman in the same store
Charles Laughton:	hotel front desk attendant
Jerry Lewis:	hotel bellboy
Malcolm McDowell:	coffee salesman
Ali MacGraw:	editorial assistant on the magazine *Harper's Bazaar*, the American edition
Steve McQueen:	travelling fairground barker
Dean Martin:	hotel croupier
Walter Matthau:	filing clerk
Burgess Meredith:	newspaper reporter
Marilyn Monroe:	a stripper at the Mayan burlesque theatre in downtown Los Angeles, under the name of Marilyn Marlow
Yves Montand:	barman
Kenneth More:	fur-trapper in Canada
Jack Nicholson:	once worked in the cartoon department of MGM
Kim Novak:	part-time lift operator
Jack Palance:	professional boxer
Valerie Perrine:	stripper in a Las Vegas club act
Dick Powell:	worked for the American telephone company
William Powell:	also worked for the telephone

	company; they never met until they became actors
Basil Rathbone:	insurance door-to-door salesman
Ronald Reagan:	radio sports announcer
Oliver Reed:	bouncer for a strip club in London's West End
Michael Rennie:	car salesman
Burt Reynolds:	professional player for the Baltimore Colts
Thelma Ritter:	department store telephone operator
Roy Rogers:	ran a shoe factory
Jane Russell:	chiropodist's assistant
Margaret Rutherford:	highly respected piano teacher
Telly Savalas:	worked for the American State Department
Randolph Scott:	male model, sometimes nude
George Segal:	worked in his own jazz band
Norma Shearer:	played the piano in the theatre before the main movie
Alastair Sim:	tailor
Barbara Stanwyck:	gift-wrapped customers' purchases in a department store
Rod Steiger:	civil servant
Gloria Swanson:	sold ladies' fashions in a leading department store
Terry-Thomas:	worked in a grocer's shop
Raquel Welch:	cocktail waitress
Edward Woodward:	worked for a sanitary engineering company in the UK.

☆

Intimate Details

Lana Turner has no eyebrows. In 1938 movie mogul Sam Goldwyn ordered her to shave them off for *The Adventures of Marco Polo* and they never grew back.

☆

Ben Turpin, a famous silent screen comedy star, had crossed eyes, which became his trademark. He had them insured with Lloyds of London for one million dollars against their ever becoming normal.

☆

Jane Russell, who shot to fame in *The Outlaw*, dismissed accusations that she enlarged her bosom in the 50s movie by stuffing tissues down her bra. The movie's eccentric millionaire producer Howard Hughes insisted she wore a wired uplift bra during shooting. Jane said, 'I was wearing a jersey blouse which showed the seams of my bra and Howard wanted to avoid that. But the bra he made was agony to wear and, although no one dared tell him, I just threw it away. What I finally did was to cover the seams on my own bra with Kleenex. People said I stuffed some inside too, but that's not so.' All his life Howard Hughes thought Jane wore the bra he designed.

☆

Famous tattoos:

Glen Campbell has a dagger on his arm.

Pearl Bailey has a heart on her leg.

Joan Baez has a flower on the small of her back.

Ringo Starr has a half moon and a shooting star on his arm.

Melanie Griffith has a pear on the left cheek of her rear end.

☆

Sometimes handicaps only serve to make people more determined to succeed. Actors are no exception. Here's a list of a few who have never let their disability hold them back from stardom:

Dudley Moore was born with a club foot.
Stevie Wonder has been blind from birth.
Lou Ferrigno lost 65 per cent of his hearing as a child.
Sylvester Stallone had a nerve on the left side of his face severed as he was being born. His left side is still slightly paralysed.
Elizabeth Taylor has seen her way through thirty-odd serious illnesses since she was a child star.
Sammy Davis Jr. had a glass eye.

☆

Mae West always wore white, she thought it made her look pure and innocent. She had it written into her contract that she was the only one allowed to appear in white.

☆

Fired by Universal Studios because his Adam's apple stuck out too far was a young actor called Clint Eastwood.

☆

The following stars are/were all lefthanded: Lennie Bruce, Charlie Chaplin, W.C. Fields, Judy Garland, Cary Grant, Goldie Hawn, Marilyn Monroe, Robert Redford.

☆

For the role of Michael Corleone in *Godfather III*, Al Pacino had his dentist file down his teeth and apply a yellowish stain to them, to give more credibility to his role as an elderly man. After shooting was completed Al had his teeth capped.

☆

American television producer Mark Goodson is so particular about his appearance that when he's staying in Los Angeles he sends all his shirts back to New York to have them washed and ironed by his favourite laundress.

☆

Hollywood's largest chest in 1918 belonged to Elmo Lincoln, the first movie Tarzan – it measured 53 inches when fully expanded.

☆

Humphrey Bogart got his scarred lip when a World War I prisoner he was transporting lashed out and smashed him in the mouth. It's rumoured that Bogey then shot the man with a .45.

☆

It's been rumoured around Hollywood that the following stars may have had a little help with remodelling their noses: Dean Martin, Eva Gabor, Zsa Zsa Gabor, Carolyn Jones, Peter Jones, Stephanie Powers, Sissy Spacek, Rita Moreno, George Hamilton, Joel Grey, Nanette Fabray, Joan Hacket, Jill St John, Raquel Welch, Marlo Thomas, Annette Funicello, Barbara Eden, Phyllis Diller, Dinah Shore, Vera Ellen, Al Jolson, Cameron Mitchell, Mitzi Gaynor, Rhonda Fleming, Cher, Judy Garland and Clark Gable.

☆

In 1968 Anthony Quinn had to shave his head for the role of a Greek magician in the movie *The Magus*. He was so worried that his hair wouldn't grow back that he made the studio take out an insurance policy against this happening. He need not have worried; his hair grew back thicker than ever.

☆

After *Gone With the Wind* (1939), Vivien Leigh told the press that she would never make another movie with Clark Gable unless he remedied the foul odour which came from his dentures. She said doing the love scenes with Clark was most unpleasant.

☆

Actor George Hamilton is such a health fanatic that he has his blood cleansed regularly. He also has a thing about wearing a pair of socks twice; he never washes them, simply throws them away and replaces them with a new pair.

☆

Most people in Hollywood thought that William Boyd, who played Hopalong Cassidy, dyed his hair white to look even more dramatic in his jet black get-up. In fact his hair turned white when he was twenty-nine.

☆

Beautiful Jane Seymour has one brown eye and one green eye.

☆

When Bing Crosby was staying at the posh White Sulphur Springs Hotel in Virginia, he would hand wash all his shirts before he sent them to the hotel laundry. He did not want the laundry staff to see his dirty washing.

☆

Edward G. Robinson spoke eight languages fluently; it became a hobby of his.

☆

Yul Brynner still had hair when he made his first picture, *Port of New York* (1949). He shaved his head completely to play the King of Siam in the Broadway musical *The King and I* in 1951, and stayed as bald as a billiard ball until his death in 1985. He did wear wigs in *The Buccaneer* (1958), *The Sound and the Fury* (1959) and *Solomon and Sheba* (1959).

☆

Marlene Dietrich is thought to have got her classic sunken cheek look by having her upper rear molars removed.

☆

It's said that Marilyn Monroe wiggled her rear because she was slightly bowlegged. This made her hips sway, so she emphasized her gait by sawing ¼ inch off the heel of her right shoe. Later the movies cashed in on her wiggle, and every young woman in the 1950s was trying to walk like Marilyn.

☆

Singer Johnny Cash always wears jet black when he performs; he even has it written into his contract.

☆

The most famous nose in Hollywood belonged to Jimmy Durante; he had it insured for $250,000.

☆

Mae West is said to have massaged her breasts every night with cocoa butter to keep them firm.

☆

Joan Crawford's face and most of her body were covered in freckles. She hated them and covered them with makeup.

☆

Sandy Duncan and Rex Harrison are both blind in one eye.

☆

When singer Julio Iglesias first visited Los Angeles he was convinced the LA water was ruining his hair, so he had five gallons of pure filtered water flown in from his Miami home for shampooing only.

☆

Harold Lloyd, comedian of the silent screen, was missing the index finger and thumb on his right hand. He wore latex rubber fingers to disguise the fact.

☆

Hollywood's 'Brazilian Bombshell', Carmen Miranda, was not Brazilian; she was born in Marco de Canavezes, Portugal, in 1909. It was known around Hollywood that she never wore panties under her skirt. She said it gave her more freedom of movement when she danced. One freelance photographer took some very low angle pictures of her dancing, which revealed all. The pictures were instantly circulated everywhere, and her career was brought to an end by a number of women's morality groups hounding 20th Century-Fox Studios. They dropped her contract.

☆

Katharine Hepburn has always had a thing about clean hair. It's rumoured that she would sniff her leading man's hair to see if it smelt clean before she would do any close-up scenes with him.

☆

Buddy Epsen was originally selected to play the Tin Man in *The Wizard of Oz*, but the silver makeup gave him a skin complaint.

☆

Patrick Swayze hates his smile; he says it's lopsided. Over the years as an actor and a champion dancer he has broken his ribs, his left knee (five times), ankle, foot, and all his fingers. He says he'd like to be remembered as a perfect Southern Gentleman.

☆

Famous for his sky-blue eyes, Paul Newman is colour blind.

☆

Jason Robards Jr. was in a car accident and needed five operations to reconstruct his face.

☆

Gary Cooper has impaired hearing as a result of a dynamite blast.

☆

In 1947 Jack Palance broke Marlon Brando's nose accidentally while they were stage fighting in the play *A Streetcar Named Desire*. Marlon has never had his nose straightened.

☆

In *The Wizard of Oz* Judy Garland wore extra dark makeup on the bridge of her nose to improve the appearance of her snub nose.

☆

Ronald Reagan has been partially deaf for many years, ever since a fellow actor let off a gun next to his ear while they were filming on set.

☆

It's believed that Hollywood makeup artists used to pin back Bing Crosby's cauliflower ears with spirit gum.

☆

Peter Falk has a glass eye.

☆

In their teens both Doris Day and Lucille Ball were in very bad car accidents. The doctors thought neither of them would ever walk again because of their serious leg injuries.

☆

Producer/director Howard Hughes would never allow himself to be x-rayed.

☆

It's reported that John Travolta spends about $50 a day on lotions and restorers to combat his receding hairline.

☆

Stacy Keach, star of TV's 'Hammer' detective series, wears a moustache to hide a scarred upper lip, the result of four operations to repair a hare lip.

☆

Bhupat Giri, an Indian movie producer, is different from any other producer in the world because he is blind.

☆

John Wayne wore a hairpiece. His hair started to fall out after he contracted a virus in Korea.

☆

Lynn Redgrave was confined to a wheelchair until she was six, due to an acute case of anaemia.

☆

Jayne Mansfield once held the record for the largest bust in Hollywood, measuring 39½ inches. Today Dolly Parton is said to hold the record at 40 inches, although she will only admit to her bust being 'somewhere in the low forties'. She once said, 'When women's lib started I was the first to burn by bra and it took three days to put out the fire.'

Hollywood Wit

When Christopher Plummer was asked what it was like working with Julie Andrews in *The Sound of Music*, he said, 'Working with her is like being hit over the head with a Valentine card.'

☆

Howard Hughes, who gave Jane Russell her start in movies, once said, 'There are two good reasons why men will go to see her.'

☆

W.C. Fields, known for his drinking, revealed: 'I never drink water; I'm afraid it will become habit forming.'

☆

Joe Franklin once asked Barbra Streisand how much she'd charge to haunt a house. Barbra was not amused.

☆

Cher, asked what she thought made her sexy: 'I don't know how to make sex appeal. If anybody asks me how I do it, I tell him I don't know how I do it, I just do it.'

☆

Jane Fonda: 'Working in Hollywood does give you a certain expertise in the field of prostitution.'

☆

Dolly Parton: 'Age is only mind over matter. If you don't mind, then it doesn't really matter.'

☆

Miss Piggy, asked about her diet: 'My diet motto is – only eat as much as you can lift.'

☆

Leading Hollywood divorce lawyer Marvin Mitchelson once said, 'If you think it's expensive supporting your wife, try *not* supporting her.'

☆

Groucho Marx once joked about Doris Day, saying that her ass was so firm you could play a game of bridge on it. He also said that he'd known her before she was a virgin. Doris never spoke to Groucho again.

☆

When Mae West signed a contract with Paramount Studios she told the Hollywood press, 'I'm the girl that works at Paramount all day and Fox all night.'

☆

When Raymond Burr was asked the secret of his success he replied: 'I'm not that good an actor, but I have the strength of an ox, and I'll outlast everybody.'

☆

Julie Andrews: 'Sometimes I'm so sweet even I can't stand it.'

☆

Joan Rivers made lots of cruel remarks about Elizabeth Taylor's weight problems in her night club act. When asked about these remarks, she said, 'Liz Taylor should be very grateful to me; my jokes are one of the reasons she went on a diet. Besides, it was very embarrassing when I took her to Sea World. Shamu the whale jumped out of the water and she asked in a loud voice if it came with vegetables.'

☆

American TV talk show host Oprah Winfrey, asked how wealth and fame had changed her: 'My feet are still planted firmly on the ground, they are just in more expensive shoes.'

☆

Bill Cosby, asked for his thoughts on sex education for children: 'Sex education may be a good idea in the schools, but I do not believe the kids should be given homework on the subject.'

☆

Raquel Welch was asked on a live TV chat show to identify her 'most erogenous zone'. For a split second she was taken aback – then, to the delight of the studio audience responded, 'The brains'. She went on to say, 'I love being a world-famous sex object. But I had to do a live show to show everybody I was more than just a cash register with glands!'

☆

When Michael J. Fox was asked if being short had hindered his acting career, he said, 'You know what the difference between a short actor and a short star is? The short actor stands on an applecart, and the short star has them dig ditches for everybody else!'

☆

On accepting her Oscar for Best Supporting Actress in *A Patch of Blue* in 1965, Shelley Winters said, 'I want to thank my director Guy Green who understood the role better than I did.' She played a lush and a whore in the movie.

☆

'For a long time I kept wondering if my fly was open,' Tom Cruise said when a reporter asked him about his insecurity about people staring at him.

☆

Movie mogul Sam Goldwyn coined the phrase, 'A verbal contract isn't worth the paper it's written on.' Since then many Hollywood directors and producers have used the line as a joke.

☆

Carol Burnett: 'Doing a movie is like being pregnant; you've got that terrible long wait to see if it's ugly.'

☆

Comedienne Lily Tomlin once prophesied: 'There will be sex after death – we just won't be able to feel it.'

☆

When Marlene Dietrich was approached to endorse a product on TV, she said, 'I would never do a TV commercial, it totally destroys the star's image. The most ludicrous thing I ever saw was John Wayne dressed as a cowboy sitting on a horse, praising the effectiveness of a headache powder.'

☆

Elizabeth Taylor: 'A diamond is the only ice that keeps a woman warm.'

☆

Fred Astaire: 'I just put my feet in the air and move them around.'

☆

Cecil B. De Mille: 'Give me a couple of pages of the Bible, and I'll give you a picture you'll never forget.'

☆

Tony Curtis said, after doing a kissing scene with Marilyn Monroe in *Some Like it Hot*, 'It's like kissing Hitler.'

☆

Katharine Hepburn, asked how she viewed her huge success as an actress, replied, 'My greatest strength is, and always has been, common sense. I'm really a standard brand – like Campbell's tomato soup.'

☆

Dorothy Parker: 'Scratch an actor and you'll find an actress.'

☆

Bette Davis once said of Joan Crawford: 'The best time I ever had with Joan Crawford was when I pushed her down the stairs in *Whatever Happened to Baby Jane?*'

☆

When Victor Mature applied for membership to the Los Angeles Country Club, he was told, 'We don't accept actors.' Victor quickly replied, 'I'm no actor, and I have sixty-four pictures to prove it.'

☆

Shelley Winters: 'It was so cold I almost got married.'

☆

When Zsa Zsa Gabor was asked how she saw her ideal man, she said: 'I vant a man who only has to be kind and understanding. Is zat too much to ask of a multi-millionaire?'

☆

When Cary Grant was asked about Mae West, the woman who put him into movies, he said: 'I don't have fond memories of her. She did her own thing to the detriment of everyone around her. I do not admire superficiality.'

☆

The song 'Somewhere Over the Rainbow' was almost cut from *The Wizard of Oz*. As Judy Garland once laughingly put it, 'The MGM executives thought it would take up too much time with this little fat girl singing.'

☆

Alfred Hitchcock: 'Actors should be treated like cattle.'

☆

When Barbra Streisand prepares for a movie, she really goes all out. To research her role as a prostitute in *Nuts*, she visited a brothel in Los Angeles to see at first hand what went on. One businessman spotted her as she stood in the bordello's foyer, and asked the madam, 'OK – so how much do you want for the Barbra Streisand lookalike?' The madam said the lookalike was not one of her girls and found the man someone else.

☆

The dancer Josephine Baker once said of Maurice Chevalier, 'He is a great artiste but a small human being.'

☆

Rex Harrison played Henry Higgins in *My Fair Lady* for three years on the stage, but initially was not asked to play the role in the movie version, so he went to his house in Spain for a long holiday. One night, director George Cukor phoned from Hollywood to ask Rex if he would fly to California for a 'photographic test'. Rex, a very experienced movie actor, replied 'Absolutely not. If you want me to play the role, then I'll come', and hung up. Soon after, a friend took some joke Polaroids of him, stark naked on a beach. Rex sent them over to Hollywood with a note saying, 'If you want a photographic test, this is it.' He got the role by return phonecall from George.

☆

On the calling card of Esther Williams you will find the words 'Yes, I still swim.'

☆

Bob Hope: 'There'll always be an England ... even if it's in Hollywood.'

☆

Zsa Zsa Gabor: 'Husbands are like fires, they go out when unattended.'

☆

Joan Collins, asked for her thoughts on beauty: 'The problem with beauty is that it's like being born rich and getting poorer.'

☆

In *Crimes and Misdemeanors*, Woody Allen claimed that 'the last time I was inside a woman was when I visited the Statue of Liberty.'

☆

In Hollywood there is a lot of upstaging, but the best bit of upstaging ever was by Jayne Mansfield, who showed up very early to a press party for Jane Russell's new movie *Underwater* wearing a very skimpy bikini. As soon as Jayne jumped into the pool, her bikini conveniently snapped undone. The next morning's papers carried a picture of Jayne in the pool, along with a story. She wasn't even in the movie.

☆

Debbie Reynolds, asked to describe how she saw Hollywood: 'For a movie star ultimately there really is no such thing as Hollywood, it's a name, and it's a map. It's not an industry, it's a very fickle business where you're here today and gone tomorrow, after one hell of a ride.'

☆

Years after her childhood career had finished, an interviewer asked Shirley Temple Black why she thought she was so successful as a child star. She replied, 'I was in a class with Rin Tin Tin. People were looking for something to cheer them up, so they turned to a dog and a little girl.'

☆

Bette Davis said that Joan Crawford wore three sets of breasts – small, medium and large – through *Whatever Happened to Baby Jane?* (1961) which they made together. For the final scene on the beach Joan wore her large set. 'I had terrible trouble dragging her along the sand, it was like I was climbing over mountains. Nobody, no matter how well endowed they are, has breasts which stick up in the air when they are lying flat on their back.'

☆

Comedian Rodney Dangerfield: 'If it weren't for pickpockets, I'd have no sex life at all.'

☆

The outspoken actress Tallulah Bankhead once said, 'It's the good girls who keep diaries, the bad girls never have the time.'

☆

Woody Allen: 'I'm a practising heterosexual, but bisexuality immediately doubles your chances for a date on a Saturday night.'

☆

Errol Flynn: 'They've great respect for the dead in Hollywood, but none for the living.'

☆

Mae West: 'I do all my writing in bed; everybody knows I do my best work there.'

☆

While on location, director D.W. Griffith gave the direction: 'Move those ten thousand horses a little to the right.'

☆

Barry Humphries, the master of Dame Edna Everage, was once banned by an airline after he pretended to throw up in flight into a sick bag. He then asked the hostess for a spoon and fork, and proceeded to eat the contents of the bag. The other passengers were horrified; they didn't know that Barry had secretly emptied a Russian salad into the bag before take-off.

☆

Gene Kelly, asked why he had taken up dancing, replied, 'I got started dancing because I knew that was one way to meet girls. Then I found out that it was good for a hell of a lot more – like being a movie star!'

☆

Alfred Hitchock: 'Conversation is the enemy of good wine.'

☆

Oliver Reed, asked what it was like to co-star with the beautiful Raquel Welch in *The Three Musketeers*, said: 'She doesn't attract me. I'd rather sleep with her hairdresser.'

☆

Mickey Rooney once lamented, 'I was a fourteen-year-old boy for thirty years of my life.'

☆

Tallulah Bankhead, modestly to a newspaper reporter: 'I'm as pure as the driven slush.'

☆

Orson Welles: 'Everybody denies I am a genius, but nobody ever called me one.'

☆

Funny lady Phyllis Diller said she was once so wrinkled that she could screw her hat on.

☆

Mae West: 'Give a man a free hand and he'll run it all over you.'

☆

When gender-bender Boy George was asked by a reporter what he would like to be reincarnated as, he replied, 'Matt Dillon's underwear.'

☆

Alfred Hitchcock: 'Always make the audience suffer as much as possible.'

☆

Zsa Zsa Gabor: 'I never hated a man enough to give him his diamonds back.'

☆

Richard Pryor, asked what he thought of the movie industry: 'The movie businessmen don't care if you mess your life up, as long as you don't die during the making of a film.'

☆

Bette Midler to a rude fan: 'What are you going to do for a face when King Kong asks for his bum back?'

☆

While appearing on a TV chat show in Australia, Eva Gabor dodged several questions about her age. Towards the end of the interview the host again brought up the subject. This time Eva snapped back, 'Ordinarily I do not answer any questions about age, but since it seems so important to you, I'll tell. I am 102, Zsa Zsa is 104, Magda is 106, and mother – well she is somewhat older.'

☆

Orson Welles: 'Hollywood's all right, it's the pictures that are bad.'

☆

When Spencer Tracy was asked what he looked for in a good script, he replied, 'Days off.'

☆

Zsa Zsa Gabor is a genius of the one-line quip. Here are a few of her memorable views on marriage and sex:

'Divorce? I've always been a housewife – I always kept the house.'

'What do I think of condoms? It depends what's in it for me!'

'Darlink, I always give back the ring after a divorce, but I keep the stone.'

'I know nothing about sex because I was always married!'

☆

After Bette Davis and Joan Crawford had finished filming *Whatever Happened to Baby Jane?* (1961) the studio wanted them to do a promotional tour across America. They were to split up for personal appearances, covering 150 cinemas, but Joan protested that Bette had been given the best cinemas and dropped out of the tour. Bette jumped in and did the entire tour by herself. During it, she told a TV interviewer how hard it had been for the producers to raise the money for the film, as no one in the industry wanted to back a movie starring 'two old broads'. A few days later Bette received a very stiff handwritten note from Joan, telling her in no uncertain terms not to refer to her as an 'old broad'. From that day onward, their relationship was never the same.

☆

Being daddy one moment, then superstar Dame Edna Everage, can be a bit confusing for young children. When Barry Humphries' son Oscar was asked once what his father did, he replied very proudly, 'He's an actress.'

Firsts

Traffic Crossing Leeds Bridge (1888) was the first motion picture film. It was made by the Frenchman Louis Aimé Augustin Le Prince.

☆

Actor Van Johnson gave Elizabeth Taylor her very first screen kiss, and afterwards he said she had onions on her breath.

☆

Silent screen star Ben Turpin was the first movie actor to have a pie thrown in his face. He was starring in a Keystone Cops movie at the time.

☆

Hollywood's very first movie première was held at the Egyptian Theater in 1922. The movie was *Robin Hood*, starring Wallace Beery, Alan Hale and Douglas Fairbanks Sr.

☆

Hollywood captured the first screen kiss, lasting thirty seconds, in the 1896 movie aptly named *The Kiss*. This scene, along with a couple of others, can be seen in *The Spiral Staircase* (1946).

☆

1933 saw the first teaming of Fred Astaire with Ginger Rogers, in *Flying Down to Rio*.

☆

The first movie shot in Hollywood was *The Straw Man*, made in 1913 by Cecil B. De Mille, Samuel Goldwyn and Jesse Lasky. It cost $15,000 and earned more than $250,000, which was then a great deal of money.

☆

Sam Lucas was the very first actor to play a lead in a movie. It was *Uncle Tom's Cabin* (1914), a silent movie.

☆

Who's Afraid of Virginia Woolf? (1966) was the first Hollywood movie to use four-letter words and go out on general release. Elizabeth Taylor won an Oscar for Best Actress in it. It is listed in the Oscar Pictorial History as the film that broke Hollywood taboos for adult material.

☆

On the Beach was the first film to première simultaneously in major cities throughout the world, on 17th December 1959.

☆

Spencer Tracy narrated the first Cinerama fiction movie *How the West was Won* (1963).

☆

The stage show *Oh, Calcutta* opened off-Broadway in 1969, bringing full-frontal nudity to the American stage for the first time.

☆

Omar Sharif's second movie, in 1953, was the Egyptian production *The Blazing Sun*, the first Arabic movie to show two people kissing.

☆

The Wizard of Oz was shown for the first time in East Germany on 31st December 1989 at East Berlin's historic Babylon Theatre. The movie was first released in American in 1939, the year war broke out in Europe.

☆

Dr No (1964) was the first James Bond movie with Sean Connery as superspy 007.

☆

Gone With the Wind was shown in the Soviet Union for the first time in 1989.

Westerns

The star of the very first Western was Buffalo Bill Cody, with none other than Thomas Edison running the camera. The movie was shot on location in New Jersey.

☆

Hopalong Cassidy was one of America's first TV cowboys. In the show's heyday, 2,500 products carried the Hoppy name. Hatmaker B. Stetson & Company paid Hopalong $53,000 to have their hats carry the Hopalong Cassidy autograph and name. In one year alone in the 1950s Hopalong clothing totalled $60 million. In the late 50s, the Hopalong Cassidy empire was said to be worth some $200 million.

When his horse Topper died in 1960, followed three weeks later by the death of his groom, William Boyd – who played Hopalong – took these events as an omen. Disaster, he told his wife Grace, comes in threes. 'I'm not going to be the third one,' he said, and promptly hung up his saddle. He spent his later years living very quietly in his favourite place, Palm Desert, California. In 1972, at the age of seventy-seven, looking about fifty, he died of a brain tumour.

☆

Old-time movie cowboy star Tex Ritter once ran for the US Senate in Tennessee in 1970.

☆

Silent Western star William S. Hart posed for the original Uncle Sam poster for World War I.

☆

Burt Reynolds made his TV debut playing a halfbreed Indian blacksmith in the series 'Gunsmoke'. It was a non-speaking part; all he did was to pound the anvil and look very busy.

☆

Singing cowboy movie star Gene Autry was the first artist to record the song 'Rudolf the Red-Nosed Reindeer'.

☆

The role of Hopalong Cassidy was first offered to David Niven, who turned it down at the last minute. Both Lee J. Cobb and Robert Mitchum made their acting debuts as bit players in Hopalong Cassidy pictures; Robert went on to appear in eight Hopalong movies.

☆

Cowboy star of the silents and early talkies Tom Mix, who made one hundred Hollywood movies between 1911 and 1917, was killed in a car crash in 1940, at the age of sixty. He was buried in his white ranger coat, white riding breeches, hand-stamped boots, and a belt buckle that spelled TOM MIX in diamonds.

☆

The day Frances Octavia Smith turned fourteen, she eloped. A year later she gave birth to a boy, then at seventeen she became a widow. Today we know her as Mrs Roy Rogers – Dale Evans. In 1967 she was given the award 'Mother of the Year for California'. This famous 1940s screen cowgirl, who made many movies with her husband, admitted in a recent interview that she's always been a lousy horsewoman.

☆

Movie star Gene Autry was the first Californian cowboy to star in a TV series – it was the Gene Autry Show.

☆

On 24th June 1949 the first episode of 'Hopalong Cassidy' was shown on American TV. He galloped on to the screens that Friday afternoon, three months before 'The Lone Ranger' and just three days ahead of 'Captain Video'.

Cartoons

Walt Disney's *Snow White and the Seven Dwarfs* (1937) was the first full-length animated feature film ever made.

☆

Mel Blanc, the voice of Bugs Bunny since his first cartoon *A Wild Hare* (1940), was allergic to carrots all his life.

☆

Walt Disney took a trip to New York in 1927 to negotiate a new contract for an animated series he'd created about a character called Oswald. On arrival Walt found that the name Oswald had already been copyrighted, so he renamed Oswald Mortimer, who eventually became Mickey Mouse, the world's favourite rodent.

☆

Marilyn Monroe was the actual model type that Walt Disney used for his cartoon character Tinkerbell in *Peter Pan* (1953).

☆

Walter Lanz created the cartoon drawings of Woody Woodpecker, and his wife Grace is Woody's voice, which is speeded up a little on tape. His laughter comes from Mel Blanc's voice.

☆

In 1990 a drawing of Mickey Mouse done by Walt Disney in 1935 sold for $110,000, which made it the third most expensive animation art drawing ever sold. It was sketched in black ink on a large sheet of white paper and signed 'Best Wishes from Mickey Mouse and Walt Disney'. He did the sketch at a Hollywood party in a matter of a few seconds to amuse his guests.

☆

Mark Hamill, who rocketed to stardom as Luke Skywalker in *Star Wars*, was the voice of Flipper and the Jeannie in the 'I Dream of Jeannie' Cartoon TV series.

☆

The TV cartoon show 'The Flintstones' is heard around the world in twenty-two different languages, and syndicated in eighty countries. Not bad for a 1960s series they said would never last.

☆

In 1928 Walt Disney made his first Mickey Mouse movie in colour.

☆

In *Anchors Aweigh* (1945), Gene Kelly danced with a cartoon mouse as his partner, the first human and cartoon dance segment filmed.

☆

Mickey Mouse's voice during the first twenty years of his life was that of Walt Disney himself.

☆

Donald Duck's girlfriend made her debut in *Donald Duck* (1937), billed as Donna Duck. It was not until a few years later that she changed her name to Daisy Duck.

☆

The most used voice in Hollywood belongs to Mel Blanc; he's been doing cartoon voices half his life. He's the voice of Bugs Bunny, Daffy Duck, Porky Pig, Barney Rubble, Sylvester, Tweety Pie and over 200 more characters.

☆

In May 1989 at Christie's East Auction Rooms, a cel (with a production background) from a 1934 Walt Disney short was auctioned for $286,000 to an anonymous Canadian collector. Back in 1934, how many people who saw the black-and-white movie *Orphan's Benefit*, which features Mickey Mouse and one of the first appearances of an irritable, frequently victimized duck named Donald, could have known that a single moment of it would be worth so much in 1989?

☆

During the movie slump of 1938 Mae West commented, 'The only picture to make money recently was *Snow White and the Seven Dwarfs*, and that would have made twice as much if they had let me play Snow White.'

☆

When cartoonist Bob Clampett saw Clark Gable eat a carrot in *It Happened One Night* (1934), it gave him the inspiration for the cartoon character of Bugs Bunny. Prior to Bugs' debut in *A Wild Hare* (1940), he was called Happy Rabbit.

Four-Legged Friends

Around the World in 80 Days (1956) holds the record for the movie using them most animals: 3,800 sheep, 2,448 buffalo, 15 elephants, 6 skunks, 4 ostriches, 800 horses, 512 monkeys, 950 donkeys and 17 bulls. The movie also had 42 cameo appearances by well-known actors and actresses.

The animal most often seen in Hollywood movies and TV series is a dog. Second most common is a horse, third a cat, then come chimps, lions, tigers and then seals.

In the Hollywood epic *Quo Vadis*, shot in 1925, one of the lions killed an extra on the set. The attendants were very reluctant to shoot the beast because the cameras were rolling and they did not want to spoil the scene. But when the lion started to eat the extra, the producer gave the order to shoot.

Only two animals have their own star on Hollywood's Walk of Fame; Rin Tin Tin and Lassie.

There were three Totos used in *The Wizard of Oz*. First was a female Cairn terrier named Terry, accidently injured when one of the Wicked Witch's guards stepped on her. A second dog filled in for several days, and the third was supposedly a stuffed toy dog used for extensive camera and lighting test shots.

☆

Beauty is a popular name for horses in the movies; Joan Crawford rode one in *Johnny Guitar*; Clark Gable's horse was called Beauty in *Lone Star*, as was Elizabeth Taylor's horse in *Giant*.

☆

In 1926 Rin Tin Tin was voted most popular movie star. At the first Academy Awards ceremony the dog scooped the pool with the most votes for Best Actor Oscar. He was eliminated by the panel of judges, making way for a German actor called Emil Jannings, who won the first Academy Award for Best Actor in 1928.

☆

While filming *Doctor Doolittle* (1967) Rex Harrison was bitten by a chimp, a duck, a dog and a parrot. He is now a strong believer in never working with animals or children.

☆

In *The Wizard of Oz* a dozen actors played the flying winged monkeys. Clever camera work and hundreds of miniature rubber monkeys made it seem as if there were thousands of them.

☆

For *Planet of the Apes* (1968) the makeup budget came to $1 million, 17 percent of the total production cost. Seventy-eight makeup artists worked on the movie, and head makeup man John Chambers won a special Oscar for his ape makeup design.

☆

Nick Nolte ate real dog food in *Down and Out in Beverly Hills* when he showed the dog how to use a dog bowl.

☆

The dog Lassie was receiving $1,000 a week at the height of its career. In Lassie's contract it was stated that there be a fully air-conditioned kennel on standby twenty-four hours a day, along with a personal hairdresser. Lassie was really a he, but he was replaced with a she in *Lassie Come Home* (1943).

☆

Rock wildman Alice Cooper always performed on stage with his favourite boa constrictor Monty, until Monty died after being bitten by the mouse he was eating for breakfast. A few weeks later Alice's other snake, Yvonne, disappeared down a hotel lavatory.

☆

In an episode of TV's 'MacGyver' they sawed off the horn of a rhino, and the TV production company received thousands of letters complaining that this was illegal. Then the truth came out; it was a very realistic-looking mechanical rhino-head which cost the production company $40,000.

☆

In *The Godfather* the horse's head in the bed was a real one.

☆

The dashing snow-white stallion Topper, who galloped his way through the Hopalong Cassidy movies sixty-odd years ago, is buried in the Los Angeles Pet Memorial Park in a specially made casket nine feet long and seven feet wide. William Boyd, who played Hopalong, gave specific instructions about where his beloved horse should be buried. Over the years a number of visitors to the pet cemetery say they have seen Topper trotting through the tombstones. The caretaker says the sightings and stories are more than just wild imagination; he too has seen Topper more than once.

☆

Elizabeth Taylor: 'Some of my best leading men have been horses and dogs.'

Oscars, and Other Awards

Up until 1931 the Academy Award trophy – a figure of a man with a Crusader's sword standing on a reel of film – was simply called the Statuette. Then in January 1931 Margaret Herrick, an Academy librarian, just chanced to remark, 'He looks a lot like my uncle Oscar', and from that minute on the nickname stuck.

☆

The very first Academy Awards presentation was held in the Blossom Room of the Hollywood Roosevelt Hotel on 16th May 1929.

☆

Walt Disney received the most Oscars in the history of the Academy Awards. In all he was presented with twenty-six gold statues.

☆

Deborah Kerr and Thelma Ritter have been nominated six times each for an Academy Award, but neither has ever won. Richard Burton holds the record to date for the performer with the most nominations (seven in all) who never has won an Oscar.

☆

When Julie Andrews gave her acceptance speech for her Best Actress Oscar for Mary Poppins in 1964, she said, 'You Americans are famous for your hospitality, but this is ridiculous!'

☆

The Best Picture Academy Award in 1927 went to *Wings*, the only silent movie to win such an award.

☆

Movie Art Director Cedric Gibbons designed the Oscar award in 1928. It stands 13½ inches high, and is cast of solid Britannia metal electroplated with 18-carat gold. It weighs 8½ pounds. The Dodge Trophy Company in California makes the statuettes at a cost of £200 per Oscar. No Oscar is ever meant to be sold; it must first be offered back to the Academy of Motion Picture Arts and Sciences.

☆

Only two actors have been awarded an Emmy, Oscar, Tony and a Grammy Award; Liza Minnelli and Rita Moreno.

☆

Bette Davis upset all Hollywood by turning up at the very formal Academy Awards show in 1935 wearing an informal dress.

☆

In 1926 the uncle of Grace Kelly, George Kelly, won a Pulitzer Prize for drama.

☆

One of the most touching moments at any Oscar ceremony was when Louise Fletcher signed along with her moving acceptance speech. She is the daughter of deaf parents, and said she wanted to tell them of her 'special gratitude'. Jill Ireland presented Louise with the Oscar for Best Actress for *One Flew Over The Cuckoo's Nest* (1975).

☆

James Cagney's sister Jeanne appeared with him in *Yankee Doodle Dandy*, for which James won an Oscar for Best Actor in 1942.

☆

At the age of six, Shirley Temple won a special Oscar Award for her outstanding contribution to screen entertainment during 1934. But Tatum O'Neal is the youngest person to receive a regular Academy Award; she was nine when she won the Oscar for Best Supporting Actress for her role in *Paper Moon* (1973).

☆

Richard Dreyfuss was the youngest winner ever of the Best Actor Oscar. He received it in 1977 for his performance in *The Goodbye Girl* when he was twenty-nine.

☆

The only tie for Best Actress Oscar was in 1968, between Barbra Streisand for *Funny Girl* and Katharine Hepburn for *The Lion in Winter*.

☆

When the nodules on Frank Sinatra's throat brought his singing career to a temporary standstill, he accepted a small fee of just $8,000 to star in *From Here to Eternity* (1953). The role gave him an Oscar as Best Supporting Actor.

☆

After Charlie Chaplin and Orson Welles, Sylvester Stallone was the third Oscar nominee for acting and script writing his first movie, *Rocky*.

☆

In 1942 Greer Garson won an Oscar for Best Actress in *Mrs Miniver*. But what people remember most is her forty-minute acceptance speech, still a record today.

☆

Jane Wyman in *Johnny Belinda* (1948), John Mills in *Ryan's Daughter* (1970) and Patty Duke in *The Miracle Worker* (1962) all won Oscars for roles as mutes. Jane Wyman's acceptance speech went like this: 'I accept this very gratefully for keeping my mouth shut. I think I'll do it again.' When John Mills stepped up to receive his award, he did not say a word.

☆

In 1966 the Golden Turkey Award for the worst performance in a movie went to singer Tony Bennett for his role in *The Oscar*.

☆

The Grammy Award is one of the music world's most prestigious awards, but over the years it has honoured the spoken word, documentary, children's stories, comedy and poetry. Among the winners have been; Martin Luther King Jr, Orson Welles, Garrison Keillor, Eddie Murphy, Jim Henson's Muppets and Bob Newhart. Stevie Wonder, holder of seventeen Grammy Awards up to 1989, has won more than any other singing star.

☆

Acting sisters Joan Fontaine and Olivia de Havilland were both born in Tokyo. Joan won an Oscar in 1941 for Best Actress, in *Suspicion*, Olivia won an Oscar in 1949 for Best Actress in *The Heiress*. They are the only sisters to have won Oscars. The only brother and sister to win Oscars were Lionel and Ethel Barrymore.

☆

Stars who have won a Tony, an Oscar and an Emmy Award are: Jack Albertson, Paul Scofield, Melvyn Douglas, Thomas Mitchell, Ingrid Bergman, Shirley Booth, Helen Hayes, Liza Minnelli, Cloris Leachman and Rita Moreno.

☆

As Henry Higgins in *My Fair Lady* Rex Harrison captured the Best Actor Academy Award in 1964. In the 1989 Queen's Birthday Honours list he was knighted, becoming Sir Rex at the age of eighty-one.

☆

Spencer Tracy and Katharine Hepburn have been nominated for more Academy Awards than any other actor or actress, Spencer nine times and Katharine eleven times.

☆

Walter and John Huston, father and son, both won Academy Awards for *The Treasure of the Sierra Madre* (1948); Walter for Best Supporting Actor and John for Best Director. This is the only time family members have won Oscars on the same evening.

☆

In 1977 when the *Saturday Night Fever* soundtrack album won a Grammy award, thirty singers, musicians and producers crowded the Grammy stage to collect the award.

☆

Up to 1989 'Bewitched' star Elizabeth Montgomery had never won an Emmy award in nine tries for five different TV programmes after some thirty-odd years in TV.

☆

Jack Benny was to co-star with Walter Matthau in *The Sunshine Boys* (1975), but he died only months before the movie was to go into production. George Burns stepped into his shoes at the eleventh hour, which gave him his only Oscar, for Best Supporting Actor. It made him the oldest star to receive this award; he was eighty at the time.

☆

Lorne Greene, born in Ottawa, was honoured with the title 'Canada's Man of the Year' in 1965.

☆

In 1984 Robert Jacobsen, internationally renowned sculptor, designed the first Danish Film Academy's Oscar, which he called Alta. He would not take any fee for the design, but asked for, and got, a free pass for life to every movie theatre in Denmark.

☆

In 1971 Jane Fonda won a Best Actress Oscar for her role in *Klute*, making her the first member of the Fonda family to win an Oscar.

☆

Academy Award winner Yul Brynner commented, on receiving his Oscar, that he was the only winner who was as bald as the statuette. He won the award for playing the King of Siam in *The King and I* (1956).

☆

John Lennon and Paul McCartney won an Oscar for Best Original Song Score in 1970 for the movie *Let It Be*.

☆

In November 1984, it was reported that a Montreal movie usher was claiming a new world record for watching boring movies. He sat through fifty-seven consecutive showings of the old Ronald Reagan feature *Bedtime For Bonzo*. He was rewarded with his very own personal copy of the movie.

☆

Sam Shepard won a Pulitzer prize for drama in 1979, for his play *Buried Child*.

☆

The Turning Point (1977) and *The Color Purple* (1986) were both nominated for eleven Academy Awards, but neither movie received an Oscar, making them the most nominated movies to receive no awards.

☆

During World War II all the Oscars given out were made of wood sprayed with gold paint. This was done to conserve metal.

☆

Melvyn Douglas, John Gielgud, Ruth Gordon, John Houseman, Helen Hayes and Dame Margaret Rutherford were all over seventy years old when they won Oscars for supporting roles.

☆

Lyricist Sammy Kahn was nominated thirteen times for an Academy Award before he won his first for the song 'High Hopes'.

☆

Hollywood's Entertainment Hall of Fame was opened in 1974. Elected as their first ten members were: George Bernard Shaw, Eugene O'Neill, Tennessee Williams, Charlie Chaplin, Judy Garland, Katharine Hepburn, Irving Berlin, Laurence Olivier, George Gershwin and D.W. Griffith.

☆

Spencer Tracy is the only actor to win Best Actor two years in a row, for *Captains Courageous* (1937) and *Boys Town* (1938).

☆

Gregory Peck won an Oscar for *To Kill a Mockingbird* (1962), which made him the first native Californian to win an Oscar.

☆

At the 1974 Academy Award show's live telecast David Niven walked on to the stage to announce his co-presenter Elizabeth Taylor, when the phantom streaker dashed behind him across the stage. 'Isn't it fascinating that probably the only laugh that man will ever get is by stripping off his clothes and showing his shortcomings', said David, dismissing the streaker. He had accomplished his 'streak' so quickly and smoothly that hundreds in the audience weren't quite sure what they had just seen. His name was Robert Opel, and he was shot to death in the San Francisco sex paraphernalia shop he owned on 9th July 1979. Two men armed with sawn-off shotguns burst through the door of his shop, called Fey Way, and killed him. All they got was five dollars out of the till, a used camera and a bit of stock.

☆

Judy Garland was the favourite to win an Oscar for her great comeback performance in *A Star is Born* (1954), but she lost the award to a newcomer called Grace Kelly for her role in *The Country Girl*. Judy never won an Oscar.

☆

Edith Head, who won eight Academy Awards for her movie designs, still holds the Hollywood record for the most Oscars for a costume designer. Before she got into the movie industry she taught French and Spanish at a girls' school.

☆

Lucille Ball was the first woman to receive the Friars Club Life Achievement Award for her numerous contributions to the field of entertainment.

☆

The Sound of Music (1965) won a Best Picture Oscar, and is one of the most popular musicals of all time.

☆

The children of Henry Fonda, Judy Garland, Kirk Douglas and Ryan O'Neal have all won Oscars.

☆

To date the only husband and wife team to have won Academy Awards for acting have been Laurence Olivier and Vivien Leigh. He for Best Actor in *Hamlet* (1948) and an Honorary Oscar in 1946, and she for Best Actress in *Gone With the Wind* (1939) and *A Streetcar Named Desire* (1951).

☆

Katharine Hepburn has won four Oscars as Best Actress: for *Morning Glory* (1933), *Guess Who's Coming to Dinner* (1967), *The Lion in Winter* (1968) and *On Golden Pond* (1981).

☆

The only person ever to be nominated for an Oscar both as Best Actor and as Best Supporting Actor was Barry Fitzgerald for his performance in *Going My Way* (1944).

☆

In 1948 Laurence Olivier directed the movie *Hamlet*. He also played Hamlet, and won the Oscar for Best Actor. Talk about directing yourself to stardom!

☆

The equivalent of the Academy Award in Germany is the Bambi; in Finland they have the Snosiki.

☆

When Helen Hayes saw herself in her first movie, *The Sin of Madelon Claudet*, she was so upset at her performance she attempted to buy the movie original from the studio so that she could destroy it. The studio wouldn't hear of it, and just as well. In 1931 Helen won the Best Actress Oscar for this role.

☆

Jacqueline Kennedy won a TV Emmy award while she was First Lady, for her TV tour of the White House in the early 1960s.

☆

Cary Grant, Rosalind Russell and Irene Dunne never won an Oscar, and Edward G. Robinson was never even nominated.

☆

In 1976 and again in 1977 Jason Robards won an Oscar for Best Supporting Actor.

☆

The most Oscars won by one picture is eleven, which went to *Ben Hur* (1959).

☆

Timothy Hutton, aged twenty, was the youngest actor to receive an Oscar for Best Supporting Actor. The movie was *Ordinary People* (1980).

☆

Four years in a row, the American Institute of Voice Teachers named Loretta Young as having the best feminine speaking voice in Hollywood.

☆

In 1973 Jack Lemmon won an Oscar for Best Actor in *Save the Tiger*. He also won the Harvard Lampoon's Worst Actor of the Year Award for the same picture.

☆

Hollywood Composer Victor Young was nominated nineteen times for an Academy Award, but won only one. In 1956 he was awarded the Oscar for Best Scoring of a Dramatic or Comedy Picture for *Around the World in 80 Days*. Sadly, Victor died four months before the ceremony, never knowing he'd won an Oscar.

☆

Spencer Tracy, Peter Finch and James Dean were all nominated for Oscars posthumously.

☆

Writer Dudley Nichols, who was a militant member of the American Screenwriters Guild, was the first person to refuse an Academy Award. He refused to accept the Best Writing Award for *The Informer* (1935).

☆

John Avildsen won the Best Director Oscar in 1976 for *Rocky*. A low-budget movie, it was nominated for nine Academy Awards and won three, for Best Picture and Best Film Editing as well as Best Director. Writer/leading actor Sylvester Stallone was nominated for two awards but won none.

☆

In November 1989 a United States judge ruled that anyone can own an Oscar statuette, Hollywood's most coveted prize. Judge Laughlin Waters ruled that the copyright on the famous figure was invalid because it had been distributed without the necessary © mark from the first Academy Awards ceremony in 1929 until 1941. This final ruling was made in a lawsuit brought by the Academy of Motion Pictures Arts and Sciences against a Chicago firm which makes Oscar-like 'Star Awards' statuettes for American corporations.

☆

In 1959 Shelley Winters won an Oscar for Best Supporting Actress in *The Diary of Anne Frank*. Shelley was so touched by Anne's story that she gave the Oscar to the Anne Frank Museum in Amsterdam. The museum is in the very building where Anne hid for twenty-five months.

☆

The only sequel to win a Best Film Oscar was *The Godfather Part II* (1974). The original *Godfather* (1972) also won the award.

☆

Rod Serling was the first creative writer to win the Peabody Award.

☆

In 1942 Irving Berlin opened the envelope at the Academy Awards ceremony and read out the winner for the Best Song in a movie. It was himself, for 'White Christmas'.

☆

The first black person to win an Oscar was Hattie McDaniel in 1939, for her wonderful performance as Mammy in *Gone With the Wind*.

☆

Alfred Hitchcock never won an Academy Award for Best Director of a movie.

☆

Walter Brennan was the first star to win an Oscar for Best Supporting Actor, in *Come and Get It* (1936).

☆

When Spencer Tracy won an Academy Award for his role in *Captains Courageous* (1937), he found his Oscar was engraved with the name Dick Tracy. Spencer never had the engraving changed; he always thought it was very funny.

☆

One Oscar was unclaimed for forty years. It was the first Academy Award for a documentary, won by *Krakatoa* (1932). Joe Rock was the producer, but at the time the Awards were announced he was in England, so there was nobody to accept the Oscar. When he returned to America some years later, he was unable to prove his entitlement to the award, as he didn't get a credit on the movie. It wasn't till mid 1973 that a document was found proving that Joe did produce the movie, and he picked up his prize.

Getting Technical

In *Singing in the Rain* (1952) milk was added to the rainwater so that it would film better.

☆

For *The Wizard of Oz*, MGM imported over 120 midgets to play the Munchkins. In some of the long shots children were also used to fill in, but this was always kept secret as they did not want to break the illusion.

☆

Universal Studios holds the record for the most overused haunted castle in movies. The medieval castle has been the backdrop for many B-grade horror films, as well as being featured in such movies as *Gypsy Wildcat* (1944), *Son of Ali Baba* (1952), *The Golden Blade* (1953), *The Veils of Baghdad* (1953), *The Black Shield of Falworth* (1954) and *The Purple Mask* (1955). The castle has become an all-purpose prop at the studio, and has also appeared in quite a few TV series over the years.

☆

1953 saw the first Cinemascope movie, *The Robe* starring Jean Simmons.

☆

The first movie in colour was *Toll of the Sea* which was made in 1922, beating the first full-length sound movie *The Jazz Singer* (1927) by five years.

☆

The 1964 movie *My Fair Lady* caused quite a problem for the costume department. The extra large hats worn by the 100 female extras in the Ascot scene were so big that an army surplus Quonset hut had to be put up on the Warner Bros lot to serve as a storage and dressing-room for that one scene.

☆

The most takes ever recorded for a single scene in a Hollywood movie were 342, for a sequence in Charlie Chaplin's *City Lights* (1931).

☆

The scene of the busy Indian railway platform sequence in *The Jewel in the Crown* was shot thousands of miles from India, at a disused railway station in Buckinghamshire.

☆

In *Psycho* (1960) Janet Leigh's blood in the shower scene was really chocolate sauce, the most realistic-looking substitute on black and white film. Neither Janet Leigh nor Tony Perkins played in the final sequence; they used lookalike stunt actors.

The chariot race scene from *Ben Hur* (1959) lasted 8½ minutes on the screen. The film won a Best Picture Oscar.

☆

In *Halloween* (1978) there was an instant on-the-spot change of direction where they quickly needed a horror mask. The only one they could get was a William Shatner mask – Captain Kirk in 'Star Trek'. The props department quickly sprayed it white, cut off the hair and used it as their horror mask.

☆

Janet Leigh was not nude in her chilling shower scene in the 1960 thriller *Psycho*; she wore a flesh-coloured moleskin bikini.

☆

King of the horror movies Vincent Price starred in the first 3-D movie ever made, *House of Wax* (1953).

☆

Alfred Hitchcock originally filmed *Dial M For Murder* (1954) in 3-D, but it was never shown as such.

☆

Crispin Glover played the father in *Back to the Future*, but when it came to making *Back to the Future II*, they had to use a stand-in for his character's long shots because the script had already been written when producers found out that Crispin didn't want to be in the sequel. They cleverly spliced in some of his scenes from the first movie along with his voice.

☆

The Kansas 'twister' in *The Wizard of Oz* was actually a thirty-five-foot-long canvas cone. It provided such effective footage that MGM used alternate takes of the Oz tornado in a couple of its later pictures.

☆

The first colour telecast of the Academy Awards was in 1966; the first technicolour non-cartoon movie was *La Cucaracha* (1934).

☆

ET, the extra-terrestrial model, had 150 separate movements. He could wrinkle his nose, furrow his brows, close his eyes, smile, walk and speak. But his vocabulary was just ten words in the movie and his sex has never been disclosed. ET was played by three models, designed and built for a total of approximately $3.5 million by Italian artist and sculptor Carlo Rambaldi.

☆

Alfred Hitchcock always liked the unusual in his movies. He made *Spellbound* (1945) entirely in black and white, except for one scene of a gun being fired, which showed the colour red for one-twelfth of a second.

☆

In 1989 when *Steel Magnolias* was being filmed on location in Louisiana, they wanted the trees to be full of beautiful Magnolia blooms. But as it was the wrong time of year for flowers, the movie company had the blooms flown in and wired to the trees during shooting.

☆

The year 1927 saw the talkies burst on to the movie screens with Al Jolson in *The Jazz Singer*. The sound in fact consisted only of three songs and a couple of lines of dialogue.

☆

The Abyss (1989) was the first movie to record scripted dialogue directly on to tape during underwater filming.

☆

When Howard Hughes made *Hell's Angels*, he really got carried away with the amount of film he used. If the movie had been shown totally unedited it would have run for 23½ days nonstop.

☆

Director Cecil B. De Mille wanted the greatest special effects in *The Ten Commandments* (1956), no matter how impossible they seemed. His special effects team built a water tank so large that the brick wall between the Paramount and RKO studios had to be pulled down to accommodate it. It held over 360,000 gallons of water tinted slightly blue. This was poured from fifteen manually controlled valves over a large concrete ramp which was 32 feet high and 80 feet long. The effect took a little over two years to build and cost $2,000,000, which in 1956 was an amazing amount to spend on a movie prop.

☆

In *The Bride of Frankenstein* (1935), Elsa Lanchester had to wear so much makeup that she had to be fed through a tube.

Whoops!

In 1959 Otto Preminger directed Lee Remick in *Anatomy of a Murder*. It was a serious movie, but he overlooked a point which has become more famous than the film. Lee Remick is seated in a café wearing a snow-white dress; a couple of seconds later she emerges from it in a pair of pants.

☆

In *Dance, Fools, Dance* (1930), actor Cliff Edwards was murdered at a subway entrance in Chicago. But there were no subways in Chicago until many years later.

☆

In *Psycho*, watch Janet Leigh closely as she lies 'dead' on the bathroom floor, and you will see her gulp twice.

☆

In *The Wrong Box*, which is set in Victorian times, you can easily see a number of TV aerials on the roofs of the houses.

☆

After only a couple of weeks shooting on *Elephant Walk* (1953), its star Vivien Leigh had a breakdown. She was instantly replaced by Elizabeth Taylor, but if you look carefully you can spot Vivien in a number of long shots, which were never retaken with Elizabeth.

☆

Emma Hamilton was set in the year 1804 in London. In the movie you hear Big Ben strike, but Big Ben wasn't built until fifty years later.

☆

In the Oscar-winning *It Happened One Night* (1934) Clark Gable leaves his motel room at 2.30am, drives around New York, writes a story for his newspaper and returns to his room, where the clock still reads 2.30am.

☆

The Prisoner of Zenda (1979) was set in the Victorian era, but as men on horseback ride towards a castle, a truck and two Volkswagen Beetles drive through the scene.

☆

If you look closely at the major love scene in *The Sheik* (1921) starring Rudolph Valentino, you will see a Cartier watch on his wrist. What sheik back then owned a Cartier watch, indeed, who had even heard of watches in that era?

☆

The movie about the great volcanic explosion of Krakatoa in 1883 was entitled *East of Java*. Unfortunately, Krakatoa is west of Java.

☆

In the movie *Jagged Edge* lawyer Glenn Close arrives in court wearing a grey suit, but during her opening arguments a few minutes later she is in a dark blue suit and white blouse. Then while questioning the first witness she appears in a brown suit and brown blouse.

☆

In *The Sound of Music* (1965), which is set in the 1930s, you can clearly see a number of orange boxes stamped 'Produce of Israel' in a market scene. The story took place more than a decade before the founding of the state of Israel.

☆

In *Triple Cross*, set during World War II, there is a scene where Christopher Plummer opens a newspaper with the bold headline 'Cost of Concorde Rises Again'. In 1943 we hadn't heard of supersonic passenger planes.

☆

In *Star Wars* Carrie Fisher plays Princess Leia. At one point Mark Hamill, playing Luke Skywalker, greets her by her real name, Carrie.

☆

In *Decameron Nights* Louis Jourdan is seen standing on the deck of his fourteenth-century pirate ship, when in the background a white delivery truck slowly makes its way down a hill.

☆

If you look carefully in *Son of Ali Baba* (1952), you will see one of the corpses in the battle scene move his arm quickly just before somebody stands on it.

☆

In *Rich and Famous* (1981), Jacqueline Bisset boards a flight on a Boeing 747. The year is 1969, quite a few years before the 747 was launched. In 1969 the plane was still on the drawing board.

☆

In *Raiders of the Lost Ark*, on the map marking Indiana Jones's journey, one country is clearly marked 'Thailand'; but the film is set in 1936 when Thailand was officially named Siam.

☆

In *The Viking Queen*, set in the time of Boudicca, a leading character is seen to be wearing a wristwatch in one scene.

☆

Singer Tony Orlando made his debut singing 'Tie a Yellow Ribbon Round the Old Oak Tree' in the 1970s on American TV. He was very well dressed except for one thing – he forgot to do up his fly.

☆

Stagecoach, the classic 1930s Western starring John Wayne, was set in the nineteenth century, but if you look carefully you will see car tyre tracks clearly visible in the desert sand during a couple of scenes.

☆

In *Cain and Mabel* (1936), during the big production number starring Clark Gable and Marion Davies, a stage hand wearing dirty overalls wanders onto the set, and exits very sheepishly after a few seconds. The producer didn't notice his screen appearance until the movie had been out for quite a few years, and it is still there.

☆

When the Wicked Witch of the East was killed in *The Wizard of Oz*, all the Munchkins were seen singing out so that the entire land could hear. But at the first screening of the movie, it was discovered they had sung 'Ding, dong, the bitch is dead'. Within twenty-four hours they had dubbed in the word 'witch' and removed 'bitch'.

☆

In *Carmen Jones*, the camera tracks its star Dorothy Dandridge down a street, and if you look in the shop windows you will see the entire movie crew reflected in them.

Exits

A few days before W.C. Fields died, a friend visited him in hospital and found him thumbing through a bible. When asked what he was doing, Fields looked up and said, 'I'm just looking for a few loopholes.'

☆

In March 1958 Elizabeth Taylor had a very bad viral infection and stayed at home instead of flying with her husband Mike Todd to a promotional evening for his movie *Around the World in 80 Days*. That night his plane crashed, killing all on board.

☆

Andy Warhol occasionally contemplated his death, and once said, 'I do like the idea of people turning into dust or sand, and it would be very glamorous to be reincarnated as a big diamond ring on Elizabeth Taylor's finger.'

☆

Ray Bolger, who played the Scarecrow in *The Wizard of Oz* (1939), was the last surviving leading actor in the cast. He died in 1987.

☆

During a live interview on a TV chat show in New York, a rambling and very incoherent Truman Capote had to be taken off the air. Among other things, he said he had slept with all his psychiatrists and would eventually probably die from a mixture of booze and pills – which certainly contributed to his death.

☆

Actor Nick Adams dubbed his voice for James Dean's in one uncompleted scene from *Giant* (1956). Dean was killed in a car accident on September 30th 1955.

☆

TV star David Janssen dreamed he saw a coffin being carried out of his Beverly Hills mansion. When he asked who was in it, he was told, 'Some actor called Janssen.' A little less than forty-eight hours later he suffered a massive heart attack and died at the age of forty-nine, at his home; he was carried out in a coffin.

☆

Thin was in vogue for every Hollywood starlet in 1925; if you weren't pencil slim you were out! That year actress Barbara La Marr died from a drug overdose, but the studio was so anxious to avoid a scandal that they put out a press statement saying her death was due to stringent dieting.

☆

Jean Harlow, who starred in *Saratoga* (1937), died before the movie was completed. Mary Dees stood in for her, and Paula Winslowe dubbed her voice.

☆

While starring in *Solomon and Sheba* on location in Spain, forty-four-year-old Hollywood hearthrob Tyrone Power died of a heart attack. He died on 15th November 1958, four weeks before the movie was finished. They used a double for long shots and the movie got out on time.

☆

'See that Yul gets star billing. He has earned it.' These were the last words uttered by Gertrude Lawrence, seconds before she died in 1952. She and Yul Brynner had been starring in the stage musical *The King and I*.

☆

'Die, I should say not, dear fellow. No Barrymore would allow such a conventional thing to happen to him.' These are rumoured to be actor John Barrymore's dying words.

☆

On 1st November 1985, comic Phil Silvers, seventy-three, was looking through his fan mail with his secretary when he excused himself to take an afternoon nap. He never awoke.

☆

Marilyn Monroe died the day before she was scheduled to give an important press conference. What she was going to say we will never know. The date was set for 6th August 1962.

☆

Jeanette MacDonald died the day before she was scheduled for open heart surgery, an operation she had been awaiting for many months.

☆

Mama Cass did not choke on a ham sandwich in 1974; she died of a heart attack.

☆

The mother of Frank Sinatra, Dolly, was killed in a plane crash in 1977, en route to see her son perform in Las Vegas.

☆

Peter Lorre died just half an hour before he was due in a divorce court.

☆

W.C. Fields, who said at every opportunity that he hated Christmas, dogs and children, died on Christmas Day 1946. Charlie Chaplin also died on Christmas Day in 1977.

☆

Ingrid Bergman died on her 67th birthday, 29th August 1982.

☆

Actress Inger Stevens, best known in her role as the Swedish housekeeper in the TV series 'The Farmer's Daughter', tried to commit suicide in 1959 when her romance with singer Bing Crosby came to an end. In 1970 she committed suicide by drug overdose, aged thirty-five.

☆

The award for the strangest suicide attempt must surely go to Paul Bern. Just before he married the 1930s sex symbol Jean Harlow, Paul, a well known movie producer of the day, tried to flush his own head down the toilet. One of his rescuers was his actor friend John Barrymore. After marrying Jean Harlow – it was a very short marriage – Paul eventually killed himself with a gun.

☆

Gig Young, Oscar winner for his role in *Teacher's Pet* (1958), killed himself and his wife in 1978.

☆

Frances Bavier, who portrayed the lovable housekeeper Aunt Bee in TV's 'Andy Griffith' show in the 60s, died on 6th December 1989 aged eighty-six, a total recluse in her Californian home. The stench from her fourteen cats, coupled with peeling plaster, frayed carpets and worn upholstery indicated that she was either unable or unwilling to spend much time keeping up the home she bought in 1972. Her cats evidently used a basement room and a shower stall as a litterbox. The actress spent most of her days in a large back room plainly furnished with a bed, a desk, a TV and two old trunks, one filled with her fan mail of years ago, the other with old studio portraits of herself. In the garage was a 1966 Studebaker with four flat tyres which had not seen the light of day for years.

☆

On 18th September 1932 at the age of twenty-four, actress Peg Entwistle jumped to her death from the letter H of the Hollywood sign. There have been reports over the years that many people have jumped to their deaths from the sign, but Miss Entwistle's is the only recorded suicide from the landmark.

☆

Irving Berlin, who died on 22nd September 1989 at the age of 101, brought the world some wonderful music; 'White Christmas', 'Cheek to Cheek', 'Puttin' on the Ritz', 'Blue Sky' and 'Always'. He was a rather crude pianist; he played only the black keys and couldn't read or write music. He used an invention called the transposing piano, which had a built in lever that moved the keyboard, changing the key signature. He was known as the Howard Hughes of show business, a paranoid, reclusive, genius tycoon. He never allowed any of his songs to be used for commercials. In 1985 director Steven Spielberg asked if he could use one of his songs in a movie. Irving said no, that he was saving his works for his own ideas. He was ninety-eight years old at the time.

☆

On 2nd October 1985 Rock Hudson died of AIDS and an uproar over love scenes hit Hollywood. Only a few months earlier Rock had played Linda Evans's lover, with an on-camera open-mouth kiss in 'Dynasty'. This prompted the American Screen Actors Guild to pass a 'kissing rule' which required producers to notify the performers in advance if a role included open-mouth kissing.

☆

When he was dying, Aristotle Onassis sent for Anthony Quinn and begged him to portray him in the movie *The Greek Tycoon*. Aristotle thought Anthony was the only actor who could portray him favorably. The two had only met once, several months before the final script was completed.

☆

When Sir Laurence Olivier died, the American TV network CBS observed a minute of silence, which is the first time an English actor has been given this honour.

☆

A little over two years after his death James Dean was still receiving fan mail; thousands of fans would not accept he was really dead. Some even wanted to dig up the body to prove it wasn't James's. For weeks after his funeral police guarded his grave around the clock.

☆

When Louis B. Mayer died his funeral was attended by huge crowds, but not because of his popularity in Hollywood. As his one-time partner Sam Goldwyn said, 'The main reason so many people turned up at his funeral was they wanted to make sure he was really dead.'

☆

Actors William S. Hart and Tom Mix were pallbearers at the funeral of the famous US lawman Wyatt Earp.

☆

Jeanette MacDonald sang 'Ah, Sweet Mystery of Life' at the funerals of movie mogul Louis B. Mayer and actor Nelson Eddie. At her own they played her recording of the song, making her the only star to have sung at her own funeral.

☆

During the last few minutes of Humphrey Bogart's funeral service, his wife Lauren Bacall placed a small solid gold whistle in the urn which held his ashes. On the whistle were inscribed the words, 'If you want anything, just whistle'. These were the lines she spoke to him in their very first movie together, *To Have and Have Not* (1944).

☆

George Reeves, who played Superman on TV, died on 16th June 1959. He was buried in the grey double-breasted suit he had worn for years as Clark Kent in the smash hit 1950s series.

☆

On 16th August 1956 Bela Lugosi died in his Hollywood apartment. As he had requested in his will, Bela was buried in the high-collared cape he wore in his many portrayals of Count Dracula. His final resting-place is at the Holy Cross Cemetery, only a few feet away from his old friend Bing Crosby.

☆

Douglas Fairbanks and Tyrone Power have the same quotation from 'Hamlet' on their gravestones; 'Goodnight, sweet prince, And flights of angels sing thee to thy rest.'

☆

A woman who bought a vacant vault right next to Marilyn Monroe's in the Westwood Memorial Park decided to put it up for sale in 1980. One man thought the prospect of spending eternity beside Marilyn Monroe was too good to miss; he paid $30,000 for the vault, about ten times the price of a similar vault at Westwood.

☆

John Wayne's epitaph is written in Spanish; it reads: 'He was ugly, he was strong, and he had dignity.'

☆

When Rudolph Valentino died in 1926, several women committed suicide and a whole nation mourned. He was buried in a magnificent silver-bronze coffin, wearing a slave bracelet given to him by his last wife, actress Natacha Rambova. He was placed in a temporary vault that belonged to his friend, the woman who first discovered him, writer June Mathis. Unfortunately the grand plans for a huge marble monument were abandoned at the last minute, and to this day Rudolph rests in his borrowed wall crypt, no. 1205 in the Hollywood Memorial Cemetery. Ironically, when he was alive he stood many times in front of his own wall crypt to place flowers on the crypt of Miss Mathis's mother Virginia, who lies just below Rudolph. June Mathis died just twelve months after Rudolph, and now lies in the wall crypt on his left.

In his will, Rudolph left his first wife one dollar, so that she could not contest the will.

☆

Errol Flynn died in 1959, and was buried in an unmarked grave until 1979. It is rumoured that he was buried with six bottles of whisky, placed in his coffin by his drinking buddies. He was fifty years of age when he died of a heart attack.

☆

Part of the cremated remains of the famous gay author Truman Capote disappeared in a macabre theft during a Halloween fifty-seventh birthday party thrown by Joanne Carson in her Beverly Hills home. Truman died in Joanne's home in 1984. Since they were close friends, she kept half his ashes; the other half went to his long-time lover Jack Dunphy. Joanne's party on Halloween fulfilled her promise to Truman, that she would give a Hollywood version of the famous masked ball he had held in 1966 at the Plaza Hotel in New York. Among the fifty-odd guests that night were Sally Struthers, Valerie Harper, Judge Reinhold, Kelly McGillis, Phyllis Diller and Alan Thicke. In the morning Joanne found the ashes missing. No report of the theft was ever filed with the LA Police Department, and to this day the ashes have not been returned.

☆

The largest and most flamboyant grave of any movie star can be seen at Hillside Cemetery in Los Angeles. It's the grave of Al Jolson, which includes an enormous statue of him on his knees in his famous 'Mammy' pose. He died in 1950 of a heart attack, aged sixty-four.

☆

Tarzan author Edgar Rice Burroughs died in 1950, leaving instructions that he was to be cremated and his ashes buried beside his mother's under the south side of the big black walnut tree in the front yard of his office on Ventura Boulevard. He buried his mother's ashes there in 1944, although she died in 1920.

☆

Peter Finch dropped dead of a heart attack in the lobby of the Beverly Hills Hotel in 1977. For almost two years, he was buried in an unmarked grave at the Hollywood Memorial Cemetery. In 1979 his widow moved him into the mausoleum across from Rudolph Valentino.

☆

Walt Disney died of cancer on 15th December 1966. The actual cause of death was acute circulatory failure, following surgery one month earlier. There have been many stories that his body has been kept on ice, as he believed that they would find a cure for cancer some day and bring him back to life. This is totally untrue. His ashes are in the corner garden of Forest Lawn Cemetery in California. The 24th December issue of the French magazine *Match* marked Walt's passing with an evocative portrait of Mickey Mouse with a tear falling from his right eye, with the headline 'Adieu à Walt Disney.'

☆

Marilyn Monroe's ex-husband Joe DiMaggio's twenty-year love ritual of having six red roses placed on her crypt three times a week ended with his death in 1982.

☆

Liberace, music's most flamboyant showman, died in 1987. He is buried at Forest Lawn Cemetery in Burbank, California, in a tomb also containing his mother and brother George. The tomb, embellished with his signature and grand piano, is located between two trees shaped like candelabra, which were his trademark for many years.

☆

Hollywood's most visited grave is Marilyn Monroe's, in the Corridor of Memories in Westwood Memorial Cemetery. Her crypt is very plain with a simple brass plaque reading: 'Marilyn Monroe 1926–1962'.

☆

Grace Kelly's family kept her tragic death a secret from her ailing mother for seven years. She died on 6th January 1990 aged ninety-one, thinking her beloved daughter was still alive. It's said that a granddaughter, Grace Levine, who looked like Princess Grace, occasionally visited Margaret Kelly and pretended to be the Princess. The family kept her death a secret from Margaret because they feared the truth would kill her.

☆

The ghost of Lionel Barrymore is the most sighted ghost in Hollywood. It is said he still walks the rooms and corridors of his last mansion on Summit Drive in Beverly Hills. John Mercedes, a writer, now owns the house and says that he and many of his guests have seen the old star wandering around the house.

Everything You Ever Wanted to Know ...

Americans went wild over the movies in 1933; a total of 80 million people went to the movies each week, paying 25¢ for adults, 10¢ for children. For this you got a double feature and the chance to win a door prize.

☆

A very wealthy Australian socialite (who will remain nameless) returned a $5,000 evening gown to an exclusive designer shop in Sydney, demanding her money back. She told the shop that the gown was meant to be a one-off, but on the evening of the day she bought it she had seen Dame Edna Everage wearing the identical dress on TV.

☆

For many years the voice of Julie Andrews could be heard in all British Airways planes instructing you in in-flight procedure.

☆

The historical character most portrayed in the movies is Napoleon Bonaparte. Between 1897 and 1988 he appeared in 177 movies.

☆

Because Elizabeth Taylor was a Jewish convert, her 1963 movie *Cleopatra* was banned in Egypt.

☆

When Nikita Khruschchev visited Hollywood in 1960 he was not allowed to visit Disneyland for security reasons. Instead, he had a private visit to 20th Century-Fox studios to see the making of their latest movie, *Can Can*. He thought the movie was disgusting.

☆

Priscilla Presley says she was never allowed to eat caviar in all the years she was married to Elvis. He hated any kind of fish food, and told her he would have her thrown out of the house if he caught her eating any.

☆

There is a larger movie industry in India than in Hollywood.

☆

In 1937 there were two child actresses in the movie listing of top ten stars; Shirley Temple was number one and Jane Withers was number three.

☆

In 1985 Bette Davis donated fifty-nine of her personal scrapbooks to the Boston University library. The University was delighted, but were amazed to find every picture of Joan Crawford in Bette's scrapbooks had her teeth blacked out. Nobody was ever game enough to ask Bette about this.

☆

At thirty-three Dustin Hoffman played the greatest age span by a single actor in a movie. In the title role of *Little Big Man* he aged from seventeen to 121.

☆

Adolf Hitler's favourite actress was Greta Garbo. He was totally besotted with her, and owned a copy of every movie she ever made.

☆

When *The Wizard of Oz* was first released in England in January 1940, it was labelled 'adults only' by the English censors because of Margaret Hamilton's expertly terrifying performance as the Wicked Witch. During World War II Australian troops in North Africa adopted 'We're Off to See the Wizard' as their marching song as they went into battle with Italy.

☆

The buxom actress Jane Russell has twin mountain peaks in Alaska named after her.

☆

Hollywood producers originally offered Sylvester Stallone $360,000 for his script of *Rocky*. They wanted Burt Reynolds to play the title role. Sylvester held out, and finally sold the movie idea and script for $75,000, with the proviso that he starred as Rocky.

☆

Alfred Hitchcock had a thing about train timetables; he loved them so much he used to memorize them.

☆

Larry Hagman's chair on the set of 'Dallas' reads 'Lawrence of Malibu'.

☆

Chesterfield cigarettes were Humphrey Bogart's preferred brand.

☆

When Johnny Weissmuller was given the part of Tarzan, he was under contract to model BVD underwear and swimming trunks. MGM wanted Johnny so badly that they had to agree to let their top stars like Jean Harlow, Joan Crawford, Greta Garbo and Marie Dressler model BVD swimwear for advertisements in order to get Johnny for the role.

☆

Over the years there have been many Hollywood Brits, like: Jacqueline Bisset, Clive Brook, Charlie Chaplin, Joan Collins, Ronald Colman, Stewart Granger, Cary Grant, Sydney Greenstreet, Bob Hope, Leslie Howard, Boris Karloff, Deborah Kerr, Elsa Lanchester, Angela Lansbury, Charles Laughton, Stan Laurel, Ida Lupino, James Mason, Roddy McDowall, Ray Milland, David Niven, Claude Rains and Elizabeth Taylor.

☆

Bob Hope never wears a watch.

☆

Hollywood's youngest movie producer was Steven Paul, who directed and produced *Falling in Love Again* (1980) at the age of twenty.

☆

Hawaii has been the backdrop for many TV shows and movies over the years: 'Island Sun', 'Magnum PI', 'The Thorn Birds' and 'Jake and the Fat Man' were all shot there for TV. Hawaii stood in for Mexico in the movie *10*, the Australian cane-fields in 'The Thorn Birds', Okinawa in *Karate Kid II*, the jungles of South America in *The Raiders of the Lost Ark*, the Caribbean in *Islands in the Stream*, and the Adriatic in the 1933 submarine movie *Hell Below*.

Burt Lancaster and Deborah Kerr's classic beach love scene in *From Here to Eternity* was shot on the shores of Hawaii. The fiftieth state also provided a backdrop for *The Caine Mutiny* with Humphrey Bogart, *Mr Roberts* with Henry Fonda, *Tora Tora Tora* and *Midway*, and the mammoth war series 'Winds of War' and 'War and Remembrance'. Elvis Presley loved Hawaii and shot three of his movies there: *Blue Hawaii*, *Paradise Hawaiian Style* and *Girls Girls Girls!* The 1950 TV detective series 'Hawaiian Eye' was all shot inside a Hollywood studio, but the 'Hawaii Five-O' series was shot on location in Hawaii, using the Breakers Hotel on Beachwalk, Waikiki, for a few scenes.

☆

On 16th November 1989 hundreds of Batman fans fluttered around a spotlight outside Tower Records in Hollywood which was casting the Bat sign high in the LA night sky above Sunset Boulevard. Around 9 pm the Batmobile rolled up and the Joker jumped out, bearing bags filled with the coveted Batvideos. The show sold 100 videos of the movie in the first forty minutes, while the movie was still playing at more than 500 theatres in North America.

☆

In a long line of acting roles Charlton Heston has played three American presidents, three saints and two geniuses.

☆

The only Hollywood movie ever to be shown on Soviet TV was *They Shoot Horses, Don't They?* (1969), which starred Jane Fonda and Susannah York.

☆

Mae West left the silver screen after *The Heat's On* (1943), and did not appear in another movie for thirty-five years, until *Myra Breckenridge* (1970). She holds the record for the longest gap in a career.

☆

Originally the climax for *King Kong* (1933) was to take place in the Yankee Stadium, but at the last minute the writers changed it to the top of the Empire State Building in New York. The movie had a working title of *The Eighth Wonder* because they wanted to keep the name King Kong under wraps until a few weeks before the launch. Fay Wray was not the first choice to play Ann Darrow; producer Merian C. Cooper wanted Jean Harlow, or second choice Ginger Rogers, for the role.

☆

At one time there was talk about making the movie *The African Queen* into a musical starring Doris Day and Lee Marvin. Bette Davis and John Mills were up to star in a British production, a couple of years before the 1951 version with Humphrey Bogart and Katharine Hepburn.

☆

In 1964 auditions were held right across America and Europe for seven young actors to play the Von Trapp children in the movie version of Rogers and Hammerstein's Broadway hit, *The Sound of Music*. Some 300 child actors auditioned, including an eighteen-year-old called Mia Farrow, who was rejected. For the movie's twenty-fifth anniversary all the children turned up in America, except for Nicholas Hammond – Friedrich – who was working on a movie in Australia.

☆

Joan Collins concedes to being famous, but says it does have a few drawbacks. She can cope with the eternal curiosity about her private life and living in the goldfish bowl syndrome, but while she was visiting the loo in a very exclusive restaurant a woman shoved a scrap of paper under her door for her autograph. Joan thought this was going a bit far!

☆

Charlie Chaplin once entered his own lookalike competition and did very well – he came third.

☆

Shirley Temple received 135,000 gifts from her admiring fans for her eighteenth birthday.

☆

Mae West was one of the very few stars listed in the Los Angeles phone directory. It was one of her little quirks; she believed her fans should always be able to contact her.

☆

To quell complaints over violence in the PG-rated hits *Gremlins* and *Indiana Jones and the Temple of Doom*, on 27th June 1984 Hollywood invented a brand new rating category: PG-13.

☆

Burt Reynolds once purchased a pair of small white gloves embroidered 'MM', which belonged to Marilyn Monroe, at a Hollywood auction for an undisclosed amount.

☆

In the 1950s Ronald Reagan and his wife Nancy did a commercial promoting house lighting for General Electric. It was shown both on TV and in the movie theatres before the big movie.

☆

Marilyn Monroe and Jean Harlow both made their last movies with Clark Gable.

☆

The Gabor sisters are three of the world's true celebrities; they are famous for being famous. So said Elsa Maxwell, who was Hollywood's partygiver of the 30s, 40s and 50s.

☆

Adolf Hitler's all-time favourite movie was *King Kong*.

☆

In 1921 Hollywood made and released 854 full-length feature movies. This record has never been broken.

☆

On 15th December 1939 *Gone With the Wind* premiered in Atlanta, Georgia. The state's governor was so happy to have the world première in his state that he declared the day an official state holiday.

☆

The poster for *Casablanca* is still the most collectable and best-selling movie poster of all time.

☆

The words 'Judy – Judy – Judy' were never said in any movie by Cary Grant; it was something invented and used by imitators as a characteristic Cary Grant exclamation.

☆

The real life Father O'Malley – Eugene F. O'Malley of Chicago – went to his grave in December 1989 at the age of seventy-eight still wondering how he became the model for the character made world famous by Bing Crosby in *Going My Way* and *The Bells of St Mary's*. He never met Bing, and the only real similarity between his life and the movie was as a priest directing a boy's choir.

☆

The studio had a clause written into Shirley Temple's contract that her hair must always have fifty-six little curls in it when she appeared in front of the cameras. Her curly top trademark was checked three or four times a day during filming by the studio hairdresser, to see that none of the fifty-six had fallen out.

☆

Diane Keaton starred in the stage musical *Hair*. She was the only cast member in any of the *Hair* production companies to refuse to take her clothes off for the nude scene.

☆

Barbie the teenage doll was created by Jack Ryan, the sixth husband of Zsa Zsa Gabor.

☆

In *The Man Who Never Was* Peter Sellers was the voice of Sir Winston Churchill.

☆

Over the years the role of Cleopatra has been portrayed by Theda Bara, Claudette Colbert and Elizabeth Taylor.

☆

During the lean years when there was no acting work coming in, Harrison Ford built a sun porch for actress Sally Kellerman. Today she has a sign on her sundeck saying 'This is the Deck H.F. Built'.

☆

According to American *Variety* magazine, Loretta Lynn's film biography *A Coal Miner's Daughter* is now ranked among the All Time Film Rental Champs on the American market. In 1989 the total number of rentals reached a staggering 35 million-plus, not counting the number of video tapes sold.

☆

Marcel Marceau, the world's greatest mime artist, was the only actor to utter a word in Mel Brook's *Silent Movie*. All he said was 'No'.

☆

In *Look Who's Talking* (1989) you didn't ever see Bruce Willis, he simply did the voice of the baby. He took no pay for his speaking role, simply a percentage of the profits.

☆

The most-quoted Hollywood movie line of 1938 was an over-the-top imitation of Charles Boyer: 'Come wiz me to the Casbah', which he is meant to have said to Hedy Lamarr in *Algiers*. In fact this line was never spoken in the movie, and nobody quite knows where it came from.

☆

In the 30s, Edward G. Robinson held the record for being the most shot-at actor. He was shot to death at the end of *Little Caesar* (1931), *Silver Dollar* (1932), *I Love a Woman* (1933), *Barbary Coast* (1935), *Bullets or Ballots* (1936) and *Kid Galahad* (1937). In fact the record still stands.

☆

Meryl Streep once called cheeky Dustin Hoffman 'an obnoxious pig', when he grabbed her breast during her audition for a Broadway play he was producing. At the time Meryl was a struggling young actress. Years later the couple went on to star together in *Kramer vs Kramer*.

☆

Danny La Rue always had a fear of aeroplanes, until he flew out to Australia and New Zealand in the late 70s. Now he thinks nothing of flying everywhere.

☆

There was never any love lost between Bette Davis and Joan Crawford. During *Whatever Happened to Baby Jane?* the two were often at each other's throats. While filming a fight scene Joan was so afraid that Bette would really hit her that she demanded they use a dummy. Joan later said that Bette managed to kick her in the head just before the dummy took over for her character. Later in the shooting Joan got her revenge when Bette had to carry her after a death scene; she wanted Bette to suffer at every step, so she wore heavy weights strapped to her body.

☆

In 1949 top Hollywood model Robin Roberts brought a lawsuit against Humphrey Bogart for snatching a giant toy panda out of her hands at the El Morocco nightclub. In court Humphrey told the judge that the toy panda was his; she said he had given it to her as a gift; the case was dismissed.

☆

In *You're in the Army Now*, Jane Wyman and Regis Toomey engaged in a kiss that lasted 3 minutes and 5 seconds, still an on-screen kiss record today.

☆

The four-letter word 'love' appears in more movie and TV titles than any other word.

☆

The largest outdoor movie set in Hollywood history was in the silent movie *Intolerance* (1916), directed by D.W. Griffith.

☆

Jamie Farr, from the M*A*S*H TV series, starred as Santini in *The Blackboard Jungle* (1955).

☆

In the early 1930s, before Bette Davis achieved stardom, she played in a commercial for the first automatic dishwasher in America made by General Electric. It was shown in movie theatres all over America.

☆

TWA flight 94 from Los Angeles to Chicago on 18th November 1950 lost two of its four engines after being only a few minutes in the air. The plane was forced to land at Long Beach, where it immediately lost its third engine and crashed through a fence. Luckily nobody was hurt. Elizabeth Taylor, Ward Bond, Nancy Olson and Glen Ford were all on board, flying to Chicago for personal appearances.

☆

Harpo Marx spoke on stage only twice in his forty-seven years in show business.

☆

American TV comedy star Milton Berle was the first man to make the list of the worst-dressed women of the year, and singer David Bowie was the second. Both thought it a great joke.

☆

The snow-peaked mountain top which has become the trademark of Paramount Studios is a picture of a real mountain in Wasatch, Utah.

☆

Zsa Zsa Gabor always calls everybody darling, because she can never remember people's names. Tallulah Bankhead was the first to use the same line, making it her trademark.

☆

The surfside embrace of Deborah Kerr and Burt Lancaster in *From Here to Eternity* (1953) has gone down in movie history as one of the most passionate love scenes ever shot.

☆

James Cagney was always being quoted as saying 'All right, you guys' and 'You dirty rat'. In fact he never said either in any of his movies.

☆

In George Cukor's *The Women* (1939) he cast 135 actresses. There were no males in the movie.

☆

In 1967 when *Hawaii*, with Julie Andrews, was shown at the Center Theater at High Point in America, the theatre manager was arrested for showing a movie which the police thought obscene. It contained scenes of chaste but bare-bosomed native girls. Under a local ordnance, which had been in force since the mid-nineteenth century, any depiction of unclad breasts was an indictable offence.

☆

In 1987 Joan Collins banned her Beverly Hills dustman from collecting her rubbish after he sold it to fans. Joan thought it a gross invasion of her privacy, so she bought a paper shredder and hired a private company to remove all her rubbish.

☆

The first scene ever shot for *Gone With the Wind* was the burning of Atlanta. The movie started shooting on 10th December 1938, and was completed a year and a day later. Author Margaret Mitchell originally wanted to call her book, which she took ten years writing, *Tomorrow is Another Day*. Producer David O. Selznick paid $50,000 for the movie rights, which at the time was a record. Fourteen screenwriters were employed on the screenplay, and seven technicolour cameras were used to get the effects for the three hour forty minute movie.

☆

From 1953 to 1957 Noel Neill played Lois Lane in the TV series 'Superman'. In the 1978 movie she played Lois Lane's mother.

☆

Bo Derek holds the record for receiving the most fan mail in the 1980s, about 50,000 letters and cards a week.

☆

In 1975 Sylvester Stallone appeared in one episode on TV's 'Police Woman', starring Angie Dickinson. He played a cop called Elmore Quincy Caddo. In one scene he asks his cop partner to call him Rocky, which is his nickname. A year later Sylvester starred in his first Rocky movie.

☆

It's a Mad, Mad, Mad, Mad World (1963), a comedy spectacular of its time directed by Stanley Kramer, still boasts the longest list of comedy stars ever to appear in one movie. They were: Terry-Thomas, Spencer Tracy, Milton Berle, Sid Caesar, Phil Silvers, Mickey Rooney, Edie Adams, Dorothy Provine, Ethel Merman, Dick Shawn, Jonathan Winters, Jim Backus, Peter Falk, Stan Freberg, Buster Keaton, Don Knotts, Joe E. Brown, Marvin Kaplan, Jerry Lewis, Jack Benny, Sterling Holloway and Carl Reiner.

There were also cameo appearances by: Eddie Anderson, Leo Gorcey, William Demarest, Alan Carney, Andy Devine, Madlyn Rhue, Norman Fell, Arnold Stang, Lloyd Corrigan, Sammee Tong, Doodles Weaver, Jack Norton, Chick Chandler, Don C. Harvey, Charles Lane, Moe Howard, Larry Fine, Nicholas Georgiade, Stanley Clements, Tom Kennedy, Roy Engel, Paul Birch, Paul Ford, Zasu Pitts, Barry Chase, Edward Everett Horton, Nick Stewart, Dale Van Sickel, Roy Roberts, Barbara Pepper and Louise Glenn.

☆

Eddie Murphy holds the Hollywood record for the highest number of swear-words in a movie. *Harlem Nights* has 262 dirty words – one every 33 seconds.

☆

In the 60s mini skirts were all the rage in Hollywood and in the movies, but they were banned at Disneyland. The gatekeepers measured the distance from a woman's knee to her hemline, and didn't allow entrance to the mini-wearers unless they ripped down their hems.

☆

In 1952 veterans groups picketed Columbia's film version of Arthur Miller's *Death of a Salesman* because Miller had refused to issue an anti-Communist statement. The feeling was that the play's protagonist, Willy Loman, was a rotten salesman, not the victim of a hard-hearted system.

☆

No movie made in Japan before World War II was permitted to have any kissing scenes.

☆

Judy Garland's last movie was *I Could Go on Singing* (1963).

☆

Running for 849 performances, musician/comic Victor Borge has the longest running one-man show ever to play Broadway.

☆

In the 1961 movie of *West Side Story* George Chakiris played the leader of the Puerto Rican gang, the Sharks. But when the show opened in London's West End, George played the leader of the opposing gang, the Jets.

☆

Joan Crawford was so obsessed with cleanliness that she would follow guests around her house and polish over everything they touched, especially the doorknobs.

☆

When Pope John Paul I died after only thirty-four days as Pontiff in 1978, Clint Eastwood bought his Mercedes-Benz car.

☆

Humphrey Bogart refused many roles while under contract to Warner Bros. for which he was suspended eleven times. Lauren Bacall was suspended twelve times for the same reason.

☆

Michael Keaton, who starred in the 1989 *Batman* movie, wore out twenty-eight rubber bat suits during the filming, at a cost of $600,000. He ruined them doing most of his own stunts.

☆

The very distinctive licence plate 'BORG 9' belongs to Ernest Borgnine.

☆

In *The Cannonball Run* (1981) Roger Moore plays an Englishman called Seymour Goldfarb who suffers from a delusion that he is Roger Moore the actor.

☆

James Stewart has every hat he's worn in the movies since his debut in *The Murder Man* (1935).

☆

Joan Collins says the worst movie she ever appeared in was *Empire of the Ants* (1977), in which she played a Florida real estate developer threatened by giant ants.

☆

Lucille Ball smoked Chesterfield cigarettes all her life, though her TV show was sponsored by Philip Morris cigarettes.

☆

The voice of E.T. was done by eighty-two-year-old American housewife Pat Welsh, who received just $750 for her work.

☆

Singer Dean Martin has had a fear of elevators all his life.

☆

Johnny Weissmuller never said 'Me Tarzan, you Jane' in *Tarzan the Ape Man* (1932). Actually he said, 'Tarzan ... Jane.' And in *Casablanca* (1943) Humphrey Bogart never said 'Play it again, Sam.' He said, 'You played it for her, you can play it for me. If she can stand it, I can – play it!'

☆

When *The Sound of Music* was shown in Germany, the studio had to edit out most of the Nazi scenes, otherwise the movie would have been banned.

☆

James Dean only made six movies in his short career.

☆

Bud Abbott and Lou Costello once took out insurance with Lloyds of London in case any member of their audience should die laughing.

☆

In 1979 *The Muppet Movie* was cut by the New Zealand censor on the grounds of gratuitous violence. The scene which gave them trouble showed Fozzie Bear being menaced by a drunken sailor with a broken bottle.

☆

In the mid 1950s Universal Studios would not renew the contracts of Clint Eastwood and Burt Reynolds, because they thought neither actor showed any promise.

☆

Like clockwork, every day on an Alfred Hitchcock movie, at four o'clock tea would be served, no matter what. It was something Alfred insisted on with all his movies.

☆

Eccentric billionaire Howard Hughes was a fan of Sean Connery, and felt that Sean was his lookalike. He once said if they made a movie about his life he wanted Sean to play him.

☆

The following actors have also directed films: Leslie Howard – *Pygmalion* (1938); John Wayne – *The Green Berets* (1968); Charlton Heston – *Antony and Cleopatra* (1971); Denis Hopper – *Easy Rider* (1969).

☆

Butterfly McQueen, who played Prissy in *Gone With the Wind* (1939), was barred from the whites-only première. Fifty years later she was the guest of honour celebrating the movie's fiftieth birthday in December 1989.

☆

Swedish Love Games (1971) was made in West Germany by a West German movie company and had nothing to do with Sweden; in fact not one of the actors was Swedish.

☆

The Doctor and the Devil (1985) took thirty-one years to get to the screen after completion of the script. This is still a record.

☆

Producer David O. Selznick was fined $5,000 for allowing the word 'damn' (in Clark Gable's famous line) to be used in *Gone With the Wind* (1939).

☆

Dean Martin's number plates read 'DRUNKY'.

☆

On an average day in America 2,982,192 Americans go to the movies, 6,301,370 movie videos are rented and 7,490 homes are wired for cable TV.